BLICKLING HALL

THE NATIONAL TRUST

The text of this guidebook has been written by several authors.
John Newman has contributed the chapter on the Jacobean
house. John Fuggles, the Trust's libraries adviser, has written
about the books in chapter 5. The descriptions of textiles were
written by Pamela Clabburn, and Elizabeth Griffiths has
provided the historical introduction to the chapter on the park
and estate; I am also grateful to her for reading and correcting
the text as a whole. Many of the Trust's staff have given their
advice and expertise and I must also acknowledge the help
given by the staff of the Norfolk and Norwich Record Office,
and Peter Wade-Martins of the Norfolk Archaeological Unit.

In most of the showrooms blinds are used to protect the
ancient textiles and paintings from the damaging effects of light.
It is hoped that visitors will understand that this protection
is essential if future generations are to be able to enjoy the
rooms and their contents.

John Maddison, *Historic Buildings Representative*

First published in Great Britain in 1987 by the National Trust

Copyright © 1987 The National Trust
Registered charity no.205846
Reprinted with corrections 1989, 1993; reprinted 1992
ISBN 0-7078-0086-2

Photographs: The British Tourist Authority page 12; Richard
Bryant pages 23, 47 (left); Horst Kolo/The National Trust pages
9 (above), 11, 19, 32, 33, 38, 39, 44 (below), 45, 51; National
Portrait Gallery page 9 (below); The National Trust page 8, 10,
20, 21, 24, 27, 30, 34, 36, 43, 46 (below), 47 (right), 48, 57, 58, 59,
71, 74, 94; Norfolk Museums Service page 29; Mr Prideaux-Brune
page 28; J. Whitaker/The National Trust page 37; Mike
Williams/The National Trust pages 4, 13, 17, 18, 31, 35, 41,
44 (above), 46 (above), 50, 52, 53, 54, 55, 61, 64, 67, 68, 69, 73, 75

Designed by James Shurmer

Colour reproduction by Acculith 76, Barnet, Hertfordshire

Printed in Italy by Amilcare Pizzi s.p.a, for
National Trust Enterprises Ltd, 36 Queen Anne's Gate,
London, SW1H 9AS

CONTENTS

INTRODUCTION

'The suddenness and completeness with which the scene bursts upon the eye strikes a simultaneous chord rather than a scale of impressions: a backwater in time . . . a vanished line of Norfolk grandees, the generous vitality of Shakespeare's England, the childhood of Anne Boleyn, and, muted by the imprisoned mist of time, faint memories of famous knights, the pomp of bishops' courts, and the last of the Saxon kings passing through the water-meadows that gave his manor its name.'[1]

This heady description of Blickling was written by Christopher Hussey in 1930, two years before Philip Kerr, 11th Marquis of Lothian, decided to adopt the ancient house as his principal English seat. For many years Blickling had been let to tenants, so that Hussey's photographs that accompanied his articles showed a beautiful but rather run-down and uncomfortable old mansion, although his writing powerfully evoked the rich and romantic historical associations which had moved Sir Henry Hobart (pronounced 'Hubbard') to buy Blickling in the reign of James I. It was these associations, too, which undoubtedly fired the imagination of Philip Kerr with a desire to bring the old house back to life.

Some famous buildings, over-exposed in picture books, come as an anticlimax to the first-time visitor, but Christopher Hussey did not exaggerate: the first view of Blickling from the road will never disappoint. The warm colour of the brickwork, the glittering of its many leaded windows, the festive turrets with their gilded vanes, the extravagant gables and the outstretched arms of the wings with their dark walls of yew all contribute to an unforgettable architectural compostion.

But Blickling has not always commanded universal admiration. It was regarded with some ambivalence in the early 18th century when Thomas Wyndham of Cromer, a near neighbour who saw himself as something of a *virtuoso* in architectural matters, was moved to describe the house as 'A Chimera of Old and Young, Gay and Gloomy, a Composition of Contrarity wch never can unite to form One Pleasing Whole. What is adorned in the Modern Taste will make ye Antique Parts dark and dismal or the venerable Old Hall, Parlour etc make the new appear Gawdy and Trifling'.[2] In the valuation taken at the death of the 1st Earl of Buckinghamshire in 1756 its price was estimated chiefly in terms of the salvage of its building materials and two years later Charles Lyttelton, President of the Society of Antiquaries, called it 'a bad old house'. By now, however, it was Lyttelton rather than Blickling that

(*Left*) The house from Pond Meadow

was behind the times, for the circle of Horace Walpole was already finding much of interest and value in 'King James's Gothick'. Walpole's friend the poetess Hannah More, wrote 'You admire Houghton, but you wish for Blickling; you look at Houghton with astonishment, at Blickling with desire'.

As the putative birthplace of Anne Boleyn, Blickling had for some time possessed a certain aura of which other Norfolk houses could not boast, and if the Hall could not in the late 18th century lay claim to a great collection of works of art it had in itself become a venerable antiquity.

The alterations carried out in the 1760s and 1770s by the 2nd Earl must have been planned at exactly the time of Lyttelton's dismissive comments and are amongst the earliest instances of Jacobean architecture revived. Buckinghamshire's successors, Lady Suffield and the Lothians, were perhaps more predictably conservative in their treatment of the house, but it is an interesting phenomenon that after 1760 Blickling's powerful Jacobean character has been so carefully protected and nurtured by its various occupants.

That Blickling and its estate survive today is due entirely to the vision of Philip Kerr, 11th Marquis of Lothian (1882–1940), whose response as a Liberal to the inheritance of the title and a handful of major country houses in 1930 was circumspect. 'Largely as a result of your all too admirable work,' he wrote in reply to Lloyd George's letter of congratulation, 'a well diluted peerage is now possessed of almost no power, and I discover that I shall have to pay to our exhausted Exchequer almost 40% of the capital value of a mainly agricultural estate. In my capacity as an ordinary citizen I think highly of these arrangements but as an inheritor of a title and estates thereto they will prove somewhat embarrassing.'[3]

Lothian deprecated the merging in the national income of estate duty derived from land when agriculture itself was suffering from lack of government funding, and it was clear that great houses could not survive if their income was to be so heavily curtailed at each succession. Newbattle Abbey, his principal Scottish seat, he gave to the Universities of Scotland as an adult education college; the border castle of Ferniehurst was leased to the Youth Hostels Association. But for Blickling, which he decided to keep, he devised a special legislative solution which, in retrospect, appears to have been modelled on Lord Lee's Chequers Estate Act of 1917, by which Chequers was left to the nation for the use of successive prime ministers, with an endowment of £100,000. Lothian's use of Blickling as a place of retreat to write and to entertain academics and fellow diplomats was already broadly similar, and in 1936 he had lent the house to Stanley Baldwin for a few weeks.

Addressing the National Trust's Annual General Meeting in 1934 he set out the basis of what was to become the Country Houses Scheme, a system whereby, in place of death duties, whole houses and their contents could be left to the nation intact with their estate income as an endowment. It seemed the only possible alternative to the dismantling of Britain's country houses or their gradual erosion through tactical sales of art treasures, a process of which Lord Lothian already had painful experience in the 1932 sale of books (page 55). The bill enacted by Parliament in 1937 has been the means by which all the Trust's major houses have been saved and the process was initiated with the bequest of Blickling in December 1940. Blickling was thus the prototype for one of the most important conservation initiatives of our times. Of nearly a hundred great estates that have followed, none can displace it as the perfect representative of the English country house.

Lothian's vision extended beyond the mere preservation of architecture; he clearly saw a future for Blickling as a working house, 'a place from which public or intellectual or artistic activities go forth' as he put it. He had himself used Blickling for these purposes and there was no reason in his lifetime to anticipate that so many houses would one day be preserved for their own sake, to be visited by an increasingly mobile and informed public. Nor was it simply the house that was to be saved, for Lothian's will was quite specific that Blickling should be preserved as 'a period hall and estate'. The estate was intended to provide income for the mansion as it always had but its own character was also to be carefully fostered.

The country house divorced from its estate becomes simply a house in the country. Part of Blickling's importance is its completeness. House, garden and park are all of great quality, but the quiet and unchanged Norfolk farmland which surrounds them, with its handsome brick farmhouses and ancient cottages, its sluggish river and its dense woods, is no less precious. That is why Blickling was such a prophetic symbol for the Country Houses Scheme and why this, the first of a new series of guidebooks, attempts to deal more fully with the country house, its owners and its historical landscape.

1 Christopher Hussey, *Country Life*, 1930.

2 NNRO WKC 7/32 404 x 2.

3 J. R. M. Butler, *Lord Lothian 1882–1940*, 1960, p.145.

CHAPTER ONE

MEDIEVAL AND TUDOR BLICKING

Blickling was an old and romantic house long before its rebuilding by Sir Henry Hobart in 1619. The name, which occurs in the Domesday Book as 'Blikelinges', is now thought to indicate the settlement of the family or followers of one Blicla, although earlier this century it was thought to derive from the Old English 'Bekeling', meaning water-meadow around a stream. It is in fact in the vicinity of Moorgate in the meadows of the Bure, where the manor-house of Blickling was first built. Harold Godwinson, then Earl of the East Saxons and later King of England, owned it in the mid 11th century, transferring Blickling to his brother Gurth in 1057. At the Conquest, William I gave it to his chaplain Herfast, Bishop of Thetford, and when the see was transferred to Norwich in 1091 Blickling remained the country palace of the bishops. Bishop Everard granted the southern

(*Left*) The brass of Sir Nicholas Dagworth (d.1401); an etching by J.S.Cotman. (*Right*) Sir Thomas Boleyn (d.1539); his brass at Hever, Kent

section of the manor to John Fitz-Robert and, while the northern part remained a favourite resort of the bishops until the Reformation, Fitz-Robert's manor was to pass through many hands, in 1378 coming into the possession of Sir Nicholas Dagworth. In 1390, at the end of a distinguished military and diplomatic career in the service of Edward III, Dagworth settled at Blickling. He built a rectangular moated house, whose plan and structure was to have a powerful influence on the layout and dimensions of the Jacobean building. Dagworth died in 1401 and is commemorated by a splendid brass in the church.

Sir Thomas Erpingham, who bought Blickling from Dagworth's widow, was a man of even greater public prominence. In 1367 he crossed the Pyrenees as a companion of John of Gaunt in the ill-fated English expedition to restore the throne of Castile to Pedro the Cruel. Later his support for Gaunt's son, Henry Bolingbroke, led to his appointment as one of the commissioners to receive Richard II's renunciation of his crown.

In 1432 Blickling was bought by Sir John Fastolfe, another famous soldier whose name, sublty altered, was borrowed for Shakespeare's comic hero. At this time one of the most powerful men in Norfolk, Fastolfe owned many houses. He died at Caister Castle in 1459 having sold Blickling to his neighbour and protégé, Geoffrey Boleyn.

History has painted an unattractive portrait of the character of Geoffrey's grandson, Sir Thomas Boleyn, but he was undoubtedly one of Blickling's most interesting and significant owners. He made a place for himself at the court of Henry VIII by capitalising on the King's ardent interest in his daughters, first Mary and then her younger sister Anne. Honours were heaped on him in the 1520s: first Treasurer of the Household, then Knight of the Garter, Viscount Rochford and finally, in 1529, the earldom of Wiltshire. A patron of Erasmus, Sir Thomas led a glamorous career as soldier and diplomat. It was he who made the preparations for the historic meeting between the King and Francis I at the

The crest of Sir John Fastolfe, an early 15th-century fragment from Caister Castle, now in the Brown Room fireplace

Anne Boleyn (d.1536), a portrait from the National Portrait Gallery

Field of Cloth of Gold and Henry chose him for the unsuccessful mission to persuade the Emperor Charles V of the King's right to divorce the Emperor's aunt, Catherine of Aragon. He could hardly have been regarded as an impartial advocate and in 1533 Anne Boleyn became Queen, only to be executed with her brother three years later.

Sir Thomas died at Hever Castle, his Kentish seat, in 1539. Despite her place in history, when and where Anne Boleyn was born are not known. Tradition has always attributed her birthplace to Blickling and there is no evidence to refute this. Certainly the idea was one of the most important elements of the house's pedigree as far as the Hobarts were concerned. Ironically the 2nd Earl's remodelling of the house in the mid 18th century removed the last vestiges of Sir Thomas's Tudor range, and with it the room which had earlier been shown to visitors as the Queen's birthplace. But the 2nd Earl also reinforced the old tradition by boldly placing 'Hic Nata' below a bas-relief of Anne in the Great Hall.

After Thomas's death the property passed through his brother's hands into the possession of his relatives, the Cleres. Sir Edward Clere, who had dissipated his family's impressive wealth in ostentatious luxury, died bankrupt in 1605 and eleven years later his widow sold Blickling to Sir Henry Hobart. It must have pleased this self-made man to reflect that Shakespeare had so recently put Blickling's early owners on the London stage.

CHAPTER TWO

THE JACOBEAN HOUSE

Sir Henry Hobart came from a legal family whose most celebrated member was his great-grandfather, Sir James Hobart, Attorney-General to Henry VII. He bought the Blickling estate in 1616, but must have had his eye on it for many years. In 1590 he had been married in Blickling church, even though his bride, Dorothy, daughter of Sir Robert Bell, came from Upwell in the far west of the county near the Cambridgeshire border, and his family seat was south of Norwich at Intwood. His first acquisition of land in Blickling parish seems to have come years later in 1609.[1] However, when he at last gained possession of the Hall itself he soon set about building operations.[2] By this time he was an elderly man – his year of birth is unknown, but was probably around 1560 – and he had long been at the summit of a distin-

guished and doubtless highly lucrative legal career, including as it did the attorneyship of the Court of Wards. In 1611 he had been appointed Lord Chief Justice of the Common Pleas, and was among the first crop of baronets of the new order that was created in that year.

In London Sir Henry had a house in St Bartholomew's, Smithfield, rented from the Earl of Westmorland, and he also occupied a richly furnished suburban house at Highgate, the freehold of which he was still negotiating to purchase at the time of his death. In Norwich he leased Chapelfield House, which remained a residence of the Hobarts until the mid 18th century.

It was natural for such a man to want to perpetuate his achievements by investing some of his profits in an

Sir James Hobart (1436–1507) and his wife. A late 17th- or early 18th-century copy of a window at Loddon church

Sir Henry Hobart (d.1625), by Daniel Mytens

estate and erecting a seat in his native county commensurate with the status his abilities had won. The puzzle is that he should have waited so long. Perhaps he risked this delay because of his determination to acquire Blickling. The estate cost him £5,500,[3] a price that was little more than half the sum he subsequently spent on rebuilding. His dynastic intentions are implied by the initials carved in stone in the spandrels of some of the doorcases of his new mansion and cast in lead on the rain-water hoppers. As well as H for himself and D for his wife, there are I for his son John and P for John's wife Philippa. Yet the dates 1619 and 1620 are just as prominent on the building – these were the years in which the walls were erected and the roofs set on – as if there was also to be a permanent reminder that it was Sir Henry's generation which had established what he hoped would become a dynasty.[4]

It is also significant that Sir Henry decided not to abandon the moated site for one which, only slightly more elevated, could have given the expansive views beloved of so many Elizabethan and Jacobean builders. His decision to make use of part of the pre-existing fabric of Blickling Hall was not an exceptional one; for example, such spectacular buildings as Longleat and Audley End both incorporate monastic cloisters. But at Blickling Sir Henry also saddled his architect with considerable problems in planning the new house.

'The architect and builder of Blickling Hall' was Robert Lyminge. That is how he is described in the Blickling parish register on his death in 1629, although elsewhere he is referred to as 'your lordship's surveyor' and 'the contriver of your lordship's works'. He received a wage of 2s 6d per day during the period of construction in recognition of his role as supervisor of the works. In choosing him Hobart had gone to one of the most experienced men of the day: from 1607 to 1612

Hatfield House. Robert Lyminge completed Robert Cecil's great house in 1612, seven years before he began Blickling

The south front of Blickling

Lyminge had been employed in a similar capacity by Robert Cecil, Earl of Salisbury, in building Hatfield House, one of the most sumptuous and expensive houses of the period. At Hatfield, as Lawrence Stone has demonstrated, Lyminge suffered considerable interference from Cecil and his financial agent, as well as regularly receiving the criticisms of Simon Basil, Surveyor of the King's Works. But he learnt to stand up for himself: his response when Cecil was proposing a particularly drastic economy was 'it will be very deformed for the uniform of the build, both within and without, which I will never agree to'.[5]

The stylistic connections between Hatfield and Blickling are obvious: the angle turrets that define the bulk of the building, the shaped gables that punctuate the skyline, the entablatures that mark the floor levels and bind all the complexities of mass together. Hatfield, however, had been built on a new site. How did

Lyminge respond to the challenge of incorporating so much of the old house into his new design at Blickling?

Jacobean architecture was in many ways strongly traditional. In particular, the essential features of medieval house planning remained valid. The hall was still the kernel of the plan, entered at its 'lower' end through the screens passage, from which there was direct access to the kitchen and other service rooms. At the 'upper' end of the hall a raised dais and, normally, a bay window demarcated the area reserved for the owner and his family, even though by this time the entire household would meet and dine together in the hall only on the most festive occasions. During the 16th century two important developments had taken place. The first was aesthetic: the universal adoption of symmetry in external design, a preoccupation which was inevitably at odds with the asymmetry of the medieval plan, with its central element, the hall, entered at one end, and flanked by the unequal masses of the service rooms and private chambers. Second was the expansion of

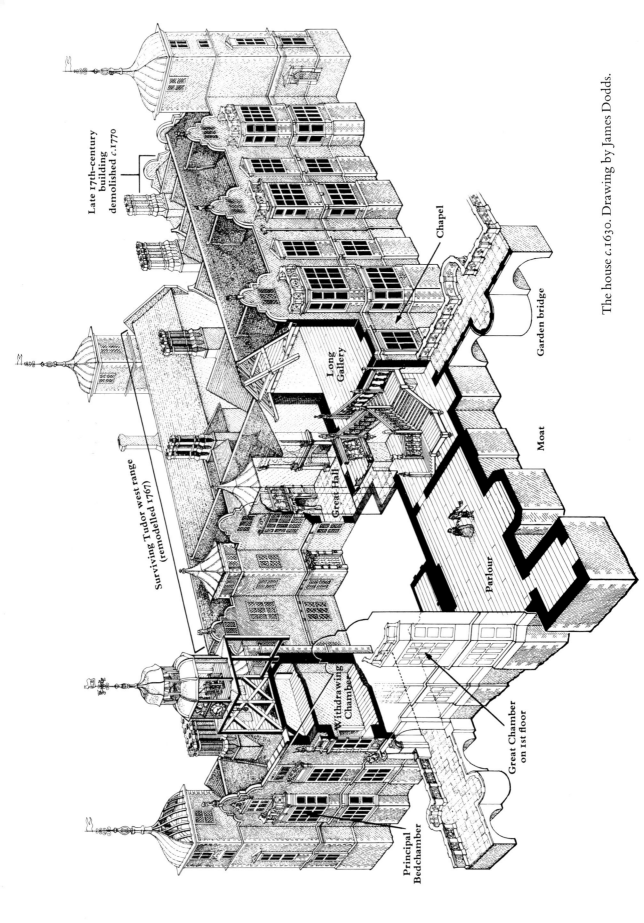

Late 17th-century
building
demolished c.1770

Surviving Tudor west range
(remodelled 1767)

Long
Gallery

Great Hall

Withdrawing
Chamber

Principal
Bedchamber

Great Chamber
on 1st floor

Parlour

Moat

Chapel

Garden bridge

The house c.1630. Drawing by James Dodds.

these private rooms, so that the great chamber and its attendant bedchamber developed into a hierarchically arranged sequence: great chamber, withdrawing chamber, bedchamber, gallery, closet; all, if possible, to form an unbroken chain.

In the west range at Blickling, where the service rooms lay, Hobart was satisfied with reroofing and internal replanning. Since the whole range was later remodelled we can only say that there were the usual rooms: servery and kitchen, with a timber screen between them, and a bridge across the moat from the kitchen; scullery, buttery, pantry, and wet and dry larders.

The parts that Lyminge was required to form into coherent architectural compositions were the south façade, the east front towards the garden and the front, or inner courtyard. Certain problems confronted him: the narrowness of the entrance front, the approach to the hall and the rest of the interior of the house through an uncomfortably tight courtyard, and access to the upper floor at a point which made it impossible to arrange the principal suite as a single sequence. In solving these problems he was led to site the main staircase in the east range so that it was approached from the hall through a lobby off the dais and thus gave room in the south-east corner of the house for a spacious parlour on the ground floor with the great chamber directly above. The withdrawing chamber which opened off the great chamber found its place in the centre of the south front above the entry passage, the principal bedchamber beyond it in the south-west angle, with a closet in the south-west angle tower. The Long Gallery could not be integrated with these three rooms and was placed on the other side of the great staircase. Here, in the east range, it could extend to the impressive length of 123 feet, and a second little closet was contrived in the north-east turret off its far end. The Long Gallery also gained a fine view of the gardens which lay on the east side of the house.

The awkward feature of this arrangement was the exposed placing of the three principal chambers across the entrance front of the house so that the view from their windows was directly into the outer court. This may have been the primary cause of the exceptionally impressive treatment of the approach to the house.

Every visitor must gasp at the first sight of Blickling Hall, framed at the end of an immense formal space between two identical service ranges, each 225 feet long and embellished with gables more elaborate than those on the house itself. Today the magnificent effect is exaggerated by the vast yew hedges which extend the space forward almost as far again; but when it was first constructed the Blickling forecourt had a different benefit: that of novelty. It was mid 17th-century designers like Sir Roger Pratt, followed by the Palladians in the 18th century, who adopted the convention of siting the service blocks to flank the house and create a complete formalised composition. Elizabethan and Jacobean designers were well used to integrating their houses with formalised garden layouts, but service buildings they normally left out of the composition. So it was a brilliant stroke of Lyminge's to use these service ranges to form a grand forecourt which both enhanced the dignity of the narrow-fronted house, and suitably distanced the principal chambers in the entrance range from the outside world. The service ranges, though they were presumably envisaged from the beginning, were not built until 1623–24 when the house itself was largely finished.

But how was Blickling Hall built? There are two aspects to this: the financial and the constructional. Hobart was in the fortunate position of being able to pay for his building entirely out of rents. In each of the three years 1619–21 his steward, Richard Burton, earmarked for the purpose rents received the preceding year. During the first two years work went ahead fast and costs were commensurately high, well over £2,000 in each year, so for 1621 Hobart set a ceiling for expenditure at a much lower level. Not surprisingly his figure of £600 was exceeded, but work did slow down sharply. In July 1625 Hobart estimated that all would be finished by midsummer the following year. However, this was a day he did not live to see. After his death in March 1626 his heir found that a number of finishing touches were required, and Lyminge himself was still being paid small sums for works in the house and garden until his death in early 1629.

At the start of building Hobart entered into a contract with a team of three master-craftsmen: Lyminge, who was a carpenter by trade, and two masons, Thomas Thorpe and Thomas Style. This was probably on 18 December 1618, when Hobart met them in London and made them an initial payment of £100. Both masons were men of considerable experience. Thomas Thorpe of Kingscliffe, brother of John Thorpe the surveyor and son of a distinguished Northamptonshire master mason, had worked for the Crown at Eltham Palace in 1603–04 and at the Banqueting House, Whitehall, the short-lived predecessor to Inigo Jones's building, in 1606–09. Thomas Style, who was probably a younger man, came to Blickling straight from executing the masonry contract for the King's Lodging in Newmarket, 1614–17. There he was working in partnership with another mason and, to judge from the royal accounts, it was a common procedure for craftsmen to enter into short-lived partnerships in order to carry out particular contracts. There is no evidence that Lyminge, Thorpe and Style had worked together before, nor do we know what made them team up for this job. Their original contract with Hobart has not survived, but they clearly undertook to execute themselves, or with sub-contractors, the masonry, carpentry and brickwork, ie the carcass of the house. Payments to the partnership were made, sometimes weekly, on the presentation of bills. This arrangement seems to have been terminated in September 1621, when Thorpe and Style must have departed leaving Lyminge resident at Blickling in sole charge of all the works.

The building costs can be assessed reasonably accurately from the accounts. The total for the house itself was just under £8,000, while the two service wings were rather more than £960 apiece. By the time Sir John Hobart, Sir Henry's son, had laid out further sums on final items of carpentry, joinery and furnishings, Blickling Hall must have cost the family over a decade something in excess of £10,000.[6]

It is possible to put this figure in some sort of perspective. On one hand the recorded expenditure on the building of Hatfield House between 1607 and 1612 amounted to £38,848.[7] Robert Cecil had, of course, erected his house at least partly as a statement of political power and it was among the costliest of the period. On the other hand is the rare surviving statement of the precise cost of a gentry house, Trentham Hall in Staffordshire, the erection of which cost Sir Richard Leveson the sum of £6,165 17s 4d between 1630 and 1638.[8]

At Blickling Sir Henry Hobart probably embarked on his building enterprise intending to be economical. That surely is one of the reasons why so much of the old house was to be retained. But his commitments in London made it impossible for him to exercise any regular personal supervision, as so many contemporary house-builders managed to do; and to let the work by contract was, in the early 17th century, far more risky than it would be today. As it turned out the contract, which was undoubtedly a detailed document, soon needed modification in two important respects, both of which pushed up costs. First, extensive areas of flooring which were to have been retained proved rotten, adding £40 to the contract price. Second, and far more significant, were the changes to the specifications, mainly more elaborate stonework, which added no less than £406 8s.

The only surviving contract, with Edward Stanyon for decorative plasterwork, establishes a rate of payment, 5s 6d per square yard, but the dimensions of the four ceilings concerned are not stated. So, without further information, Hobart would have had no idea of what the final cost would be.

During the building of Blickling the multifarious activities connected with it must have dominated the life of the village. The rumble of carts bringing in materials from all directions would have been a constant sound during the first two years. Bricks, lime, timber of various sorts, all had to be shifted short distances, while loads of stone, lead, iron and glass were arriving by sea or river and had to be carted across land the last few miles. Most of the able-bodied men of the parish seem to have been pressed into this service; no fewer than 58 are named, plus eight more from nearby villages. Admittedly, most of them were called on for just a few loads. Only William Smith was clearly in the carting business – he was paid for over 650 loads. Two others, Thomas Callow, and an Aylsham man, Walter Thompson, carried more than one hundred loads, and there were a few other regulars. One of these was the parson of Blickling, James Hargrave (page 72).

Building materials were as local as possible. Bricks were made on the estate in three specially constructed kilns, 823,000 in 1619 at 5s per thousand, 465,500 in 1620 at the lower price of 4s 6d per thousand, and in 1621–22, when the carcass of the house was largely complete, 125,000 more. Two years later the service ranges probably required a further million. The brick kilns may have been up to a mile away, for carriage of bricks was not cheap at 1s per load. Lime could also be produced locally, if an item 'for seking for lyme at Blickling'

The east front from the Parterre

implies a successful search. However, there was a more distant source of lime, costing 3s 8d per load. Sand, too, was local, for its carriage cost a few pence per load. Baskets and lime sieves were purchased in Norwich. The two lime burners were 'Allen' and William Corchever.

Timber was the other basic construction material. Firs (ie laths) could be locally supplied in their thousands. Alders for scaffold poles were available not far away at Cawston. But suitable local timber trees for floor joists, for binders in the brick walls and for the roof trusses, soon ran out. At the outset trees were viewed 'in ye parke & wood & other grounds' and by early May 1619 308 trees had been felled. The following year it was a different story: the sources of timber were Morley, presumably Swanton Morley, ten miles away to the south-west, and Langley, the estate of a Hobart relative, twice as far away beyond Norwich.

The dressed stone, an excellent oolitic Ketton type, presumably from the Thorpe family quarries in Northamptonshire, would have been shipped down the River Welland to King's Lynn and so round the coast to Cley. Paving stone from Purbeck in Dorset came in by sea to Yarmouth and so up river to Coltishall. Other materials were acquired from the best sources all over the country: lead from Derbyshire, supplied by Thomas Cryre of Hassop and Sir George Manners; iron from John Midleton of Horsham in Sussex; and Newcastle glass from Sir Robert Mansell.

Changes to the original specifications, recorded in a 'note' dated 29 November 1619, make it possible to point to a number of improvements to the design which Lyminge incorporated while work was in progress. These changes, which increased the contract price, are of particular interest because they illuminate Lyminge's approach to architectural design.[9] A major feature under discussion when the note was drafted was the wall fronting the moat before the entrance façade of the house. Lyminge pleaded against the proposed battlemented brick wall, which in his opinion 'will be very lumpish and will take away the prospect of the lower part of the house in the view of the court'. Instead he proposed 'open worke of stone', 3ft 6in high, to match the pierced stonework of the bridge, which had been cut at the quarry but was being held at the waterside until this decision had been resolved. In the end Lyminge got his way: his pierced balustrade, 'the Open Worke before the moat on the front', is costed at £47 in the note of the mason's work dated December 1620. Unfortunately this balustrade lasted for less than a century. The pierced work of the entrance bridge is all that survives now to show what it was like. Its ornamental arrow loops are the first evidence of the spurious air of military valour imparted to this lawyer's house.

The point at which a typical Elizabethan or Jacobean house made a display of the classical orders was at the entrance. A 'tower of the orders', with columns superimposed in three or even four tiers, constituted the most magniloquent piece of show possible at that period. Hatfield has a splendid example of such a tower. At Blickling the display is considerably more restrained: Doric columns flanking the entrance archway and tall banded Ionic pilasters framing the bay window above. At first an even simpler scheme was intended, nothing but the Doric columns. For Sir Henry, heraldry was doubtless what mattered here. His bull supporters surmount the piers at the outer end of the bridge and another pair stands above the Doric columns, flanking two escutcheons of his arms. A final touch to the whole composition is given by the two little statues of Justice and Prudence, suitable for a lawyer, placed on the crest of the central window bay – they came cheap at £1 each.

Originally, on the bridges spanning the moat to left and right of the entrance front, there stood compositions of triple arches with cresting. They completed the diaphanous grey stone fringe above which the red brick mansion rose.

This fringe was carried on across the garden front too, for a similar pierced stone parapet was erected here, costed, because of its great length, at £57. This, too, had disappeared before the earliest known depiction of Blickling, which dates from the 1720s, and so had a second bridge and doorway, which linked the well of the great staircase to the garden. This bridge was originally to have been of timber, but another of the extra charges listed at the end of 1619 was its construction in brick and stone. The only trace of it now is an indistinct patch in the brickwork of the east front and the brick springers of its arch (page 76).

Lyminge made two other changes to the design of the exterior of the house, both so subtle that one would hardly notice them if they were not documented, but both giving a little extra definition to the design. One concerned the tops of the turrets. Below the lead-covered turret-cap runs a full entablature, its cornice constructed of timber, the frieze and architrave of stone. The stone parts were not at first intended, and the weaker effect this would have had is demonstrated by the turrets at Hatfield, which have nothing but a cornice to crown the brickwork. The other improvement must

Hobart bulls on the entrance bridge

One of the
Jacobean newel
figures of the great
staircase

Avis, plasterer, was paid £5 for the figure of Hector.
They were in a sorry state by the middle of the 18th
century when Lord Buckinghamshire described them
shortly before their removal (page 36). The Nine
Worthies, three pagan (Hector, Alexander, Julius
Caesar), three Jewish (Joshua, David, Judas Maccabeus),
and three Christian (Charlemagne, Arthur and Godfrey
of Boulogne) had established themselves in North
European culture as epitomes of valour and virtue.
Shakespeare refers to them and several English buildings
of the period put them on show. At Montacute,
Somerset, built in the 1590s, they stand in niches high
on the entrance front, and at Aston Hall, Birmingham
(1616–30), a series executed in plaster can be seen in
decorative niches high up in the walls of the great
dining room, in an arrangement which may give some
idea of what was in the hall at Blickling.

The Worthies were warriors and leaders of men. The
military theme continued in the great staircase, which
rose in a square well in three flights, its handrail carried
on balusters linked at their feet by arcading. Every flight
was marked by a strong, high newel post crowned by a
figure, five of them in all. Against the walls were seven
half posts, with two L-shaped ones in the angles. Most
of these pieces survive in the present much enlarged
staircase, so that their original arrangement can be envisaged. At the bottom stood a post, carved on its front
face with musical instruments and a woman bearing a
lute, and on the face towards the stairwell with what
may be emblems of night: a bat, torches, a lantern on a
hanging brazier. On top stood the striding figure of a
bearded man wearing a mail collar and slashed breeches,
holding a long two-handed sword. The free-standing
post which may have stood on the first half-landing is
carved with a trophy of armour, but the figure on it, in
16th-century costume, is not military, but looks rather
more like a steward. On other newels, amid much
purely decorative carving, are a castle and a windmill.
Unfortunately none of the other figures from the newels
seems to have survived, but even so there is an air of
inconsequence and even of whimsy in the staircase
carvings.

The conception of the staircase and many details of
its carving relate it so closely to the Hatfield staircase
that Lyminge must have been responsible for both,
probably with the assistance of a specialist carver. At
Hatfield the carver's name was John Bucke; his name

also have been made to avoid another slightly dis-
appointing effect at Hatfield. There only the largest
windows, those of six lights, had a thickened central
mullion to subdivide them. At Blickling Lyminge
decided that four-light windows should also be subdivided in this way.

Internally the house was decorated with great rich-
ness and ostentation. As the visitor passed through the
screens passage into the hall he was greeted by plaster
figures of the Nine Worthies, set in niches high up in the
walls. The series was completed in 1627 when James

Detail of the plasterwork in the Long Gallery

does not occur in any of the accounts at Blickling, but then they fall silent between 1622 and May 1627, the period in which the staircase must have been constructed. All we do know is that in September 1623 Lyminge was in London, and one day went out with Lady Hobart to Hatfield. What he wanted to show her, or what contact he wanted to renew, one can only guess.

Lyminge certainly made internal features at Blickling. The openwork pendant in the centre of the staircase ceiling, of timber plastered over, was his, and so was the magnificent columned chimney-piece in the great chamber. Neither of these required the services of a carver. The chimney-piece in the parlour immediately below is scarcely less magnificent; with term figures instead of columns, it certainly needed a carver to execute the human elements. And here there is a detail which recurs on the staircase, the strings of discs which wreathe the torsos on the one and the newel-vases of the other.

Other stylistic connections lead a different way. Many of the staircase vases were carved with mask heads like those executed in stone in the courtyard doorways. These link timber-carving with stone-carving, a connection reinforced by the family likeness between the wreathed terms on the parlour chimney-piece and the wreathed terms which adorn the splendid stone doorcases, now on the hall landing but originally set at the head of the great stairs giving access to the great chamber and Long Gallery. These relationships suggest that the interior decoration was conceived as a whole,

which in the circumstances of Jacobean design may mean no more than one person, presumably Lyminge, selecting appropriate engravings for the craftsmen to work from. The mask heads, frowning or screaming, rarely calm and never smiling, are frequently met with in Jacobean carved and painted decoration and are derived from Flemish engravings, particularly those of Vredeman de Vries. But at Blickling their presence and their fierceness are particularly noticeable.

The most spectacular room in the house was the Long Gallery. The original full-height chimney-piece was removed in the mid 18th century; it was probably for this that Rowland Buckett (who had worked with Lyminge at Hatfield) gilded three pillars at a cost of £2 0s 4d in April 1624. But the glory of the room is the plaster ceiling, a dense and intricate pattern of bands enclosing heraldic and emblematic panels, the whole ceiling supported on a deep bracketed entablature. This is the first of the four ceilings by Edward Stanyon under his contract dated 11 August 1620. By the following 10 December it was finished, at a cost of £95 19s. These ceilings Stanyon was to execute 'according to such plottes & workemanship as now are or hereafter shalbe drawne by Mr. Robert Lyming his Lordshipps Surveyor of the said workes'. However, before the signing of the contract the word 'drawne' was altered to 'directed'. So what 'direction' did Lyminge give to Stanyon? In artistic terms perhaps not much. The ceiling's basic design, the broad ribs decorated with foliage trails, and strapwork motifs in every spare space, has close parallels in other houses, for example Boston Manor, Middlesex (1623) and Langleys, Essex (c.1620). They could very well all be by Stanyon. The emblematic subjects, on the other hand, are more likely to be the choice of Sir Henry Hobart, whose mantled shield of arms and motto occur in alternate panels running down the centre of the ceiling. This motto 'Quae supra', alluding to St Paul's admonition 'Set your affection on things above, not on things on the earth' (Colossians iii 2), was an addition by Sir Henry himself: in his will he calls it 'My word that I chose and use under my coate of Armes'.[10] Many great men in this period went further than this and devised their own emblems. Emblem books, beginning with Alciati's in the 1540s, were one of the most popular forms of publication all over Europe throughout the following century. The best early English example is Geoffrey Whitney's *A Choice of*

(*Right*) The Stone Court

Emblems of 1586. Among the numerous dedicatees of Whitney's 250 or so emblems are, on page 67, Miles Hobart, presumably the cousin of Intwood mentioned in Sir Henry's will. The Blickling emblems come not from Whitney, but from Henry Peacham's *Minerva Britanna* (1612), which was closely modelled on the earlier work. Peacham may have been personally known to Sir Henry and other Hobarts, for he spent the years 1613–14 in Norwich as tutor to the sons of the Earl of Arundel when they were lodging with the Bishop there. Of the 26 emblems in the gallery ceiling at Blickling all but the panels of the Senses derive from Peacham. In his preface Peacham gives an insight into the function of emblems and a reason why Sir Henry may have chosen to employ them in this particular place in his house. Emblems' true use, he says, is 'to feede at once both the minde, and eie, by expressing mistically and doubtfully, our disposition, either to Love, Hatred, Clemencie, Iustice, Pietie, our Victories, Misfortunes, Griefes, and the like: which perhaps could not have been openly, but to our praeiudice revealed'.

Peacham includes explanatory verses under each emblem, which convey their meanings – mostly didactic or otherwise improving. Those chosen for Blickling express, among other things, womanly beauty and the power of love, kingly majesty and kingly cares, divine wisdom and pity, the need to trust God and to avoid hypocrites. So an improving morning could be spent perusing the ceiling; but it must be admitted that no system is apparent in the selection and placing of the different emblems, and in one or two cases it is hard to think of a reason for their inclusion.

Off the Long Gallery, in the turret-closet, Stanyon executed a strapwork ceiling featuring the Hobart bull in the centre. At the lower rate of 4s 6d per square yard it was set down in December 1620 as having cost £3 7s 6d. After that Stanyon must have moved on to the great chamber ceiling, which closely resembles the gallery's, with broad enriched bands and fanciful pendants, with low relief strapwork patterns in the fields made by the bands. The withdrawing chamber was subdivided in the 18th century, so nothing of its 5s 6d ceiling or of its other decoration survives. The bedchamber beyond, and its turret-closet, have plasterwork ceilings of a simpler design, more like the 4s 6d work of the gallery closet. So the plasterwork established a sort of hierarchy through the rooms of the principal suite.

Doubtless their furnishings reinforced such distinctions, but unfortunately no early inventory survives to reveal how the rooms were furnished. All we know is that in 1627 Lyminge provided for the great chamber a table (page 81) and rails 'above and below' for wallhangings, presumably tapestries. The silk-covered furniture, chairs and stools, which John Baldwin, upholsterer of Norwich, was making in 1627, was intended for the 'dining chamber' ie for this room. This, too, would have been the place for Sir John to display on special occasions the rich plate bequeathed him by his father, in particular 'the greatest and most massie guilt plate' bequeathed 'for my eldest sonne, that is for my house'.

Nothing else is known for certain about how the state rooms at Blickling were furnished, but various purchases made in London when the house was nearing completion may have been intended for them. In October 1621 12 pictures of sibyls were acquired for £9 12s. Early in 1622 Christopher Jenaway, upholsterer, supplied two suites of gilt leather hangings for £49 13s, and three large pieces of tapestry hangings at a cost of £21 13s 4d. Two years later Godfrey Holmes, another upholsterer, supplied five more pieces of tapestry for £20 7s and in December 1624 Matthew Bonny, a third member of the trade, sold to Hobart for £6 13s an old piece of tapestry hanging 'of the story of Hanyball Scipio'. The most valuable of these acquisitions was also second-hand: eight tapestries depicting the story of Abraham valued at £78 and accepted by Sir Henry in July 1624 in part payment of rent arrears from Lady Fynes of Halstead House, Lincolnshire.[11]

A further especially sumptuous set of furniture reached Blickling in due course. This was the embroidered scarlet bed which, with its silk curtains, gold cups and the gilding of stools and chairs to match, cost at least £189 10s, mostly paid to Christopher Jenaway. This was a lying-in bed for John Hobart's second wife, Frances, the amply dowered daughter of the Earl of Bridgewater, whom he married in 1621. In early December 1623 she was delivered of a son and heir, christened Henry after his grandfather, who threw a magnificent christening feast in celebration. Two months later the child was dead; so it must have been with a pang that Sir Henry paid Mr Greenway the 'comfittmaker' the colossal sum of £88 in August 1624. On the other hand another delayed bill, of £3 9s paid in

The Long Gallery

April 1624 'for fringe &c for chayres and stooles suitable to the scarlet imbrothered bed against my Lady ffrances lyeing in', had to be seen as an investment for the future.[12]

On the ground floor of the east range were other important rooms. The principal family living room was the parlour. The parlour ceiling was one of the four for which Stanyon contracted at the top rate, so it is sad that the ceiling has not survived. However, the room's high status is indicated by the massive chimney-piece and overmantel bearing Sir Henry's arms and his motto 'Quae supra' in letters of especial boldness. Nothing else remains of the original arrangement of the ground floor of the east range. North of the great staircase lay the chapel, with its closet and a mysterious room called the 'yonery'. The closet was the family pew, which was framed by six carved timber arches 'to looke out of the closet to the Chapple'. A pilastered doorcase and some steps led down into the chapel, where the servants would have had their seats. In 1627 Thomas Hamline of Norwich made and installed an organ, and Lyminge made some 'garnishing' for the top of it. In the same year chairs and stools covered with green cloth were also made for the chapel. Eventually, in January 1629, the Bishop of Norwich came and consecrated it.

Beyond the chapel at the north end of the east range lay three lodgings or guest rooms. Very little is known about the north end of the house, which Hobart only remodelled and certainly did not form into a coherent range. We know there were two staircases here and between them an upper passage with an open walk below. But that is all.

Lyminge's only surviving drawing is for a covered garden seat, or 'banketting house' as he calls it. The annotations provide a few clues to the design of the Jacobean garden (page 56) and throw some further light on Lyminge as a designer. The quatrefoil loop-lights which formed a mock defence on the entrance bridge recur on the parapet of the banqueting house. There were possibly such loops at intervals along the parapet walls bordering the moat on the south and east fronts, conveying a playful air of defence throughout.

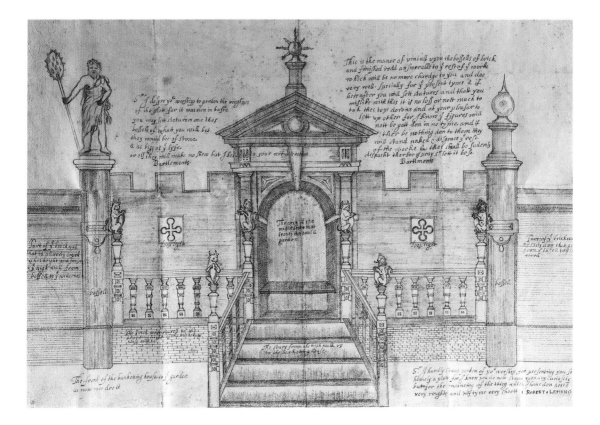

Design for a 'banketting house' in the garden, the only surviving drawing by the architect of the Jacobean house. Lyminge's annotations describe the location of the seat and suggest alternative details.

But the drawing also shows alternative ways of crowning the piers, either with statues or with ball finials. Lyminge makes it quite clear what he prefers. He wants life-size figures not mere balls, though he recognises that figures 'will nott be gott don in no tyme', so recommends the ball finials for the time being, lest while the statues are awaited the piers 'stand naked and disgrace ye rest of the worke'. He sketches in a figure of Hercules to give an idea of the effect that statues would give, notes that they may be 'of what you will', but suggests that 'they would bee of stone & as bigg as ye lyfe or els thay will mak no shew' and concludes 'but I leave it to your worshipp's discretion'.

In these remarks lies a clue to the interaction between architect and patron: Lyminge's concern was with materials and scale, but it was his employer's prerogative to suggest appropriate subjects. This is no surprise, but it helps to confirm our interpretation of the internal decoration of the house.

Sir Henry Hobart did not live to see the completion of his great house. He died in March 1626, leaving to his son the manor of Oulton to pay for the remaining building work and decoration. The bells of all the Norwich churches rang out to mark the passing of the great lawyer who, according to a contemporary, had possessed 'an excellent eloquence, the éclat of ancestry, the acutest abilities, the most engaging sweetness associated with a singular gravity'.[13]

Although Lady Hobart spent £457 on linen and other household goods for Blickling in the spring of 1624, she and her husband seem to have visited the house only once, during August that year, having first been to Cambridge where two of their sons were at St John's College.

Sir John Hobart soon established a very different pattern of living from his father's. Sir Henry had spent most of his time in London, remaining active in the practice of the law, even going on circuit each spring, until the year of his death, and his widow was established in the Highgate house.[14] Sir John's life centred on the country. The account book of his personal expenses, kept by one of his stewards, Thomas Fowler, from 21 April 1627 to 25 March 1631, demonstrates it in surprising detail.[15] This is the period when he and his family must have settled down into the new routine of life at Blickling. The annual pattern is clear: almost ten months of each year, from early July until late April, were spent at Blickling, the remaining two months in London, with a period at midsummer for leisurely travel into the country visiting friends. In 1627, for instance, the family left London on 22 June and the following night reached St Albans where they spent the next six days. Lord St John then came over and escorted them to his Bedfordshire seat of Melchbourne, where they stayed until 6 July. At their departure Sir John Hobart generously handed out over £4 in tips to the servants at Melchbourne, including the butler, the pantler, the clerk of the kitchen and four cooks, the chamberlain and the usher of the great chamber, the hall porter, sundry maids and two grooms. From there the route led, with stays of similar length but less cost, via Dodington, where there was buck-hunting and whither Sir Oliver Cromwell of Hinchingbrooke sent over strawberries, to Blickling.

Regular visitors in the following year included Lord St John, Sir Miles Hobart of Intwood, and Sir Robert Bell, of the dowager Lady Hobart's family. Their presence is betrayed when Sir John Hobart loses to them at play, at cards or at dice, and his steward has to record his losses (ranging from 5s to £1). Play invariably took place in the parlour.

The size of Sir John Hobart's household at Blickling cannot be accurately assessed. Its members were paid from quarterly sums of just over £50 given to Timothy Mathewes, the steward. Others whom Sir John on occasion paid direct include Mr Hide, his chaplain; John Mudel, his organist; and John, his page. The rest of the payments were concerned with Sir John's outdoor interests: Richard Thomas, gardener; Jonas Knight, huntsman; Francis Fiske, fowler; and a certain Baxter who on one occasion was remunerated for looking after the hawking stands.

Lady Hobart had her own allowance, of £50 per quarter, but Sir John still had to pay for expensive clothes for Frances and Dorothy, his two daughters by his first wife. Not surprisingly the buying of luxury items is recorded during the months when the family were in London, the 'great looking glasses' seen on approval on 30 May 1627 and bought for £3 the following day, and the two pictures delivered in June 1628 from the 'King's picture drawer' – possibly Daniel Mytens – of a 'kitchenpiece' and a 'gally pott of Orrange flowers'.[16]

Sir John died in 1647 leaving only daughters. The estate was inherited by the youngest of these, Philippa, who had married her first cousin, John, son of Sir Miles Hobart of Intwood. This John also inherited the baronetcy, an unorthodox arrangement emphasising the family's dynastic preoccupations in the early 17th century, preoccupations which were embodied in the building of Blickling Hall.

NOTES

1 F. Blomefield, *History of Norfolk*, III (1769), pp. 541, 603.

2 Facts concerning the building of the Jacobean house are derived from the set of accounts and estimates among the Lothian papers deposited in the Norfolk and Norwich Record Office (NNRO). This is a list of them:

(A) Accounts of Richard Burton, Sir Henry Hobart's Norfolk steward.

MC3/48 Incomplete accounts for materials delivered, 25 November 1618–24 October 1622.

MC3/43 Fair income and expenditure accounts, listing payments to craftsmen, carriage and sundries, 27 February–31 December 1619 (at f.2v plasterwork contract with Edward Stanyon, 11 August 1620).

MC3/45 Rough weekly accounts of payments to craftsmen, carriage and sundries, 4 April–25 July 1620.

MC3/49 Summary of income and expenditure to 16 May 1621 and summary of payments for materials, partly derived from MC3/48.

MC3/46 Fair income and expenditure accounts, listing payments to craftsmen, carriage and sundries, 31 December 1619–31 December 1620.

MC3/50 List of miscellaneous expenditure, 31 December 1620–16 May 1621.

MC3/47 Fair expenditure account, 31 December 1620–20 September 1621 and list of miscellaneous expenditure 20 September 1621–25 April 1622.

NRS 10191, 25, 4, 1. Summary (no details) of expenditure 1622–25.

MC3/44 Rough draft statement as at 16 May 1621.

(B) Statements of work executed:

MC3/52 Detailed notes of masons' and carpenters' work as at 29 November 1619, specifying extras to the original contract.

MC3/51 Detailed note of work done by all types of craftsmen as at December 1620.

(C)

MC3/53 Estimate, dated summer vacation 1623, for building the east office range.

The documents in B and C have been printed in full in C. Stanley-Millson and J. Newman, 'Blickling Hall: the Building of a Jacobean mansion', *Architectural History* 29 (1986), pp. 1–42, which also attempts to interpret the Jacobean fabric in the light of the documents listed here.

3 NNRO, NRS 11260, 27, D4.

4 However, the stained glass supplied by the glazier Richard Butler in February 1623 consisted of three panels only, one of the King's arms, one of Sir Henry's and one of Lady Dorothy's. NNRO Lothian additional T68A.

5 L. Stone, *Family and Fortune* (1973), p. 76.

6 The total amount received by Thorpe, Style and Lyminge between 5 December 1618 and 20 September 1621 was £2,585 7s 4d. After that date Lyminge received on his own accounts £329 13s 4d, much of which must have been for major carpentry taskwork.

The other columns of Burton's accounts are shown in the table at the bottom of this page.

For the period 21 September 1621 to 25 April 1622, itemised under sundries, the total recorded expenditure was only £197 15s 10½d.

The periodic total including the payments to the partnership and Lyminge's wages was:

To 31 December 1619	£2,518 18s 11d
To 31 December 1620	£2,187 10s 4½d
Extras (primarily iron, lead and glass) 1618–21	£ 768 17s 6d
To 20 September 1621	£ 745 8s 9½d
To 25 April 1622	£ 197 15s 10½d
1622–25	£ 943 18s 2d
Total	£7,362 9s 7½d

However, this cannot be taken as the total cost of building Blickling Hall, as statements of the cost of work done by plasterers and smiths by December 1620 tabulate works, notably Edward Stanyon's plaster ceiling in the Long Gallery, costing £96 7s 6d, certainly not covered by Burton's accounts. Presumably Hobart paid for these works direct, so that no money for them passed through his steward's hands. The surviving London accounts for 1621–25 record sundry payments for lead and glass for Blickling totalling £176 3s 4d. A figure of possibly £300 or thereabouts should be added to the recorded total. And to get a complete picture of expenditure the cost of building the two service ranges in 1623–24 must be added. The estimate of £960 for the construction of the east range suggests that they cost at least £1,000 each. The interpretation of the building accounts is made difficult by the occasional duplication of costs from one document to another. The totals stated here are therefore to be treated with some caution.

7 L. Stone, op.cit., p.91.

8 M. Airs, *The Making of the English Country House*, 1500–1640, 1975, p.82.

9 The 'note' of masons' work (MC3/52) is not signed, but as it occasionally breaks into the first person singular it is a fair assumption that it was drafted by Lyminge.

10 PRO PROB/11/148, dated 20 July 1625, proved 7 March 1626.

11 NNRO, Lothian additional T68A.

12 Ibid.

13 Judge Jenkins, 'Characters of Lord Coke and Lord Chief Justice Hobart', British Library Add. MS, 222, 629, f.225.

14 NNRO, Lothian additional T68A.

15 NNRO, NRS 14649, account book of Sir John Hobart's personal expenses, 21 April 1627–25 March 1631.

16 A galley pot was a piece of kitchen equipment generally made of glazed earthenware with a narrow neck. Commonly used for storing preserved fruit.

	1619			1620			1621 (1620 Sept)			1622–25			Total		
	£	s	d	£	s	d	£	s	d	£	s	d	£	s	d
Brickmakers	205	15	0	112	3	0	31	10	0	51	6	3	400	14	3
Limeburners	107	9	8	79	7	6	35	15	4	37	10	4	260	2	10
Firmakers	42	16	0	23	17	6	6	17	0	43	0	0	116	10	6
Purbeck pavier		—		86	13	8	15	11	0		—		102	4	8
Painter		—		18	17	7	4	0	0		—		22	17	7
Sundries	448	14	1	664	18	2	220	2	5½	125	9	3	1,459	3	11½
Smith	78	0	0	83	2	0	27	0	8		—		188	2	8
Plumber		—		33	8	0	16	0	0		—		49	8	0
Carriage	264	15	2	229	8	4	20	17	6	69	13	1	584	13	1

CHAPTER THREE

GEORGIAN BLICKLING

Within two generations of its founding, the Lord Chief Justice's monument to the Hobart dynasty had entered a period of decline. John Hobart, 3rd Baronet, who succeeded in 1647, spent much of his life engaged in bitter and expensive political contests with his Tory opponent, Sir Robert Paston of Oxnead. Hobart, who had sat in Cromwell's short-lived Upper House, was 'the idol of the dissenting and "fanatique" elements in the country', a position enhanced by his second marriage in 1656 to Mary, daughter of John Hampden. The Restoration proved only a temporary check on his career, and in 1671 a reconciliation was achieved when Charles II visited Blickling to be 'most noblie and plentifully treated in the great dining-room' (the present South Drawing Room). The King conferred a knighthood on Hobart's eldest son before departing for Oxnead where he was relieved to find himself 'safe in the House of His Friend'.[1] Hobart returned to Parliament the next year and after another decade of mutually exhausting political conflict both he and Paston expired in 1683.

Paston's death set in train the events that were ultimately to destroy Oxnead, while Hobart left his 26-year-old heir, Sir Henry, deep in debt and Blickling mortgaged to John White, a London merchant,[2] with its estate reduced to a quarter of the acreage of 1625.

John Pollexfen, another merchant to whom the mortgage of Blickling was assigned in the year of Sir John's death, was evidently used to dealing with the problems of impoverished baronets and suggested that if Sir Henry would find a lady who had between six and seven thousand a year acceptable 'he would recommend such a one'.[3] In the following year Hobart duly married Elizabeth, co-heir to Sir Joseph Maynard. A dowry of £10,000 released Blickling from its mortgage and allowed a momentary respite from financial problems.

The steward's account books for the following two decades depict a community of local people employed by the Hobarts about the house and estate. Widow Kytchen was paid quarterly 'for looking to the Rooms

and Furniture' in the hall, while John Canseller[4] waged war against rats; William Trappit[5] the gardener invoiced for tools and watering pots, and directed the labours of the women and children who weeded the beds and walks; Thomas Knowles the glazier was paid annually for keeping Blickling's many windows in good repair;[6] we hear of the bricklayers Joseph Balls and Robert Yaxley and, busiest of all, Thomas Burrows of Aylsham, the carpenter. Burrows is everywhere, moving timber barns, felling trees, building farmhouses and bridges, erecting palisades and, in the summer of 1695, making changes to the house which included the repair and modification of the east wing and moving the entrance of the Great Hall[7] (page 77). Even so, for Blickling the

Sir Henry Hobart, 4th Baronet (1658–98), attributed to William Wissing (1653–87)

late 17th century is architecturally a conspicuously quiet period. Only a panelled parlour (now the Serving Room) survives from these years. More extensive work, cleared away in the late 18th century, may, however, have been built at this time. It included a square projection with shaped gables spanning the moat on the north front and entered from the rear courtyard through an arcaded loggia. This last may have been the open walk mentioned in the Jacobean building accounts (page 26).

But the 4th Baronet was a politician rather than a builder. 'May you have many days to let them see that Sir John liveth in Sir Henry' Dr Collinges, the family chaplain, had written in 1683, adding darkly and rather superfluously 'without Pythagorean *metempsychosis*' (the transmigration of the soul of the departed into one of the living).[8] Hobart's heavy expenditure on political campaigns would, in fact, ultimately have brought Blickling to its knees but for the events which followed the election of 1698. Incensed by rumours that his decisive defeat had been brought about by allegations of discreditable conduct at the Battle of the Boyne, where he had been an equerry to William III, Hobart accused his Tory neighbour Oliver Le Neve of Great Witchingham of circulating the stories and demanded satisfaction. They met in a futile contest on Cawston Heath in

August 1698 where, contrary to expectation, the inexperienced and left-handed Le Neve managed to run his formidable opponent through. Hobart returned to Blickling to die the following day and Le Neve fled the country.[9] A simple, early 18th-century monument at Cawston bearing the cryptic inscription 'HH' commemorates this catastrophe. The ubiquitous Burrows made a coffin lined with six yards of white baize and his son spent two days cutting out the inscription. Nine escutcheons were painted for the funeral and nine gold rings bought for the bearers and the minister, John Graile, while James Norrie provided gloves of Cordova leather, fine black Spanish cloth, crape, Belledoon silk hatbands, black silk hose, fine cotton stockings and a mourning sword.[10]

The estate was put in chancery for its five-year-old heir, Sir John, and the family relinquished its position in Norfolk politics. A quiet period of slow but continuous recovery followed. Some of Blickling's most important heirlooms had been sold to trustees and in 1703 13 pictures were brought back by the steward, John Brewster.[11] They included the Mytens portrait of Lord Chief Justice Hobart and the ancient double portrait of the founder of the family, Sir James Hobart with his wife.

In 1713, having completed his education at Clare Hall,

The north front
c.1727, Edmund
Prideaux

Cambridge, Sir John Hobart set off to travel on the Continent; bills record sojourns at Lyons, Montpellier, Marseilles and Paris.[12] He returned towards the end of the following year and in 1717 married Judith Britiffe, daughter of the Recorder of Norwich. For the second time in its history Blickling was put back on its feet by a large dowry, this time of £15,000.

The Hobarts, staunch supporters of the Parliamentary faction from Civil War days, had been running with the political tide since the Revolution of 1688, and by the beginning of the 18th century the Whigs, as they were now called, had established their pre-eminence. Sir John was elected Member of Parliament for St Ives, Cornwall, in 1715 and again from 1722–27; he was MP for Norfolk in 1727–28. Meanwhile his witty and attractive elder sister Henrietta, who had made an unhappy marriage to the future Earl of Suffolk, Charles Howard, had found favour at the Hanoverian court. She became the close friend and, it was said, mistress of the Prince of Wales. Through her influence Hobart became a Knight of the Bath in 1725, Treasurer of the Chamber in 1727, and Baron Hobart of Blickling in 1728.

In the early 18th century, political ascendancy usually produced a desire to show the world the results of this power in more tangible terms: in house-building. Many of the new Whig magnates came from Norfolk families, and the county was now to witness an architectural trial of strength in which, until the 1730s, the Walpoles were the obvious victors. The luxury and grandeur of Houghton, begun in 1721, became an unmistakable expression of the authority of Sir Robert Walpole, and six years later his brother Horatio began to build at Wolterton a sober but most impressive Palladian house whose construction Hobart could almost have watched while riding in his own park. Raynham was lavishly remodelled by Lord Townshend in 1731 and Holkham begun on a gargantuan scale by Thomas Coke in 1734. The Hobarts, who had never fully recovered from the depredations of the late 17th century, could scarcely compete.

Lord Hobart's contributions to the furnishing and adornment of Blickling were, however, deliberately expressive of his place in the Whig hierarchy. His sister Henrietta's charming portrait in masquerade dress (pages 30, 86) is one of a great series (page 78) culminating in the equestrian portrait of George II (page 89) which hung originally in the Long Gallery. William Aikman

painted Hobart's friends, relatives and political allies in London in 1729. Minor gentry like Edmund Prideaux (page 28) and William Morden (later Harbord) of Gunton Hall are depicted as well as Whig grandees like Walpole, Coke and Townshend. The rich Kent frames were very much in the Whig taste and the windows of the gallery commanded a prospect of Hobart's new temple (first mentioned by a visitor in 1738[13]), identical in its proportions and details to William Kent's Holkham temple of 1729. Perhaps Kent himself was involved, or his executant architect at Holkham, Matthew Brettingham, who was later to undertake minor alterations at Blickling.[14] However, at least one important undocumented change had been made to the house before 1725. Prideaux's drawing of the

John Lord Hobart, later 1st Earl of Buckinghamshire (1693–1756), by John Heins. By kind permission of the Norfolk Museums Service

east front[15] clearly shows the large doorway in the base of the north-east turret. This proves to have been the door which originally communicated between Lord Chief Justice Hobart's stair hall and the garden, and it may be that this opening, originally off centre in the east façade, was moved because it offended the symmetry of the early 18th-century garden layout (page 76).

Hobart became Lord Lieutenant of Norfolk in 1739 and six years later, having served on the Privy Council, was created Earl of Buckinghamshire. In spite of the high offices of state which he and his successor occupied, their resources left them no leeway for the purchase of the choice works of art which were to fill other Norfolk houses at this time. But the library that came to Hobart from his distant cousin, Sir Richard Ellys of Nocton, on the remarriage of his widow in 1745, was one of the

Henrietta Howard, Countess of Suffolk (d.1767), attributed to Thomas Gibson

greatest collections of its kind and is described in detail in Chapter 5. The Long Gallery was the only room at Blickling large enough to hold 10,000 books, so the full-length portraits were dispersed to other parts of the house. A group of craftsmen set to work making bookcases and decorations; Joseph Pickford made the expensive marble fireplace; Thomas Ivory appeared for the first time, probably employed as a carpenter at this early stage in his career; Scheemakers provided a bust of Sir Richard Ellys; Francis Hayman painted a series of overdoors; and John Cheere was paid for 28 busts, 20 vases and 3 statues, presumably all of plaster.[16]

This ensemble was destroyed a century later but Hayman's paintings now hang on the Brown Stairs. The fireplace, recorded in the drawing, was a copy of one at Coleshill published by John Vardy in 1744. William Freeman, who visited Blickling in 1745, said that it was 'designed' by Lord Burlington.

But the library was the only really significant addition made by the 1st Earl, and the description of the house in the valuation taken at his death in 1756 is dismissive. 'The house is very large, all the Rooms except those in the South Front are only common useful rooms with indifferent floors, wainscot and Common Marble Chimney Pieces the foundations begin to decay and it will be a continual expense to keep it in repair. The House is of something more Value than Materials.'[17]

In some ways Blickling was a daunting prospect at this period; the gradually crumbling Tudor ranges to the north and west, with their warren of wainscotted rooms, were an obvious drawback and there were few landowners who would have warmed to the inconvenient and old-fashioned Jacobean work. It was Blickling's good fortune, therefore, that the new Lord Buckinghamshire was in tune with the most advanced architectural taste of the day, which in its enthusiasm for Gothick gladly joined turreted palaces of James I's reign with the medieval past.

John Hobart, 2nd Earl of Buckinghamshire (1723–93), having lost his mother at the age of four, spent a good deal of his childhood at Marble Hill, Twickenham, in the care of his aunt, Henrietta Howard. One of the most perfect of Palladian villas, Marble Hill was the gift of the Prince of Wales to his mistress.

Henrietta attracted the interest of some of the brightest stars of the early 18th-century Court. Dilettanti like the earls of Pembroke and Burlington were often to be

(Right) The Temple

found at Marble Hill, as were the writers John Gay, Jonathan Swift and John Arbuthnot. Her neighbour Alexander Pope was a particular friend. He helped to lay out her garden and made her the subject of four laudatory verses *On a Certain Lady at Court*. Some of those who clustered round her were disappointed that her friendship with the Prince did not secure them preferments; hence Swift's slightly cynical characterisation, '. . . an excellent companion for men of the best accomplishments who have nothing to ask'. Horace Walpole knew her later in life, when she was no longer surrounded by the acrimony of the Court, and liked her. He described the striking looks – reflected in her portrait at Blickling – which she preserved into late age, 'of a just height, well made, extremely fair, with the finest light brown hair'. She shared his enthusiasm for amusing

John Hobart, 2nd Earl of Buckinghamshire (1723–93), by Thomas Gainsborough

antiquities to the extent that in 1757 she asked one of his 'Committee of Taste'. Dr Richard Bentley, to build her a steepled Gothick farm to which she gave the spurious dedication of 'St Hubert's Priory'.

Lord Buckinghamshire was a devoted nephew and kept up a lively correspondence with her. In 1758 he wrote about an equally whimsical structure at Blickling. 'Torre del Pazzo (for such we now find by authentic records to be the ancient name of the building lately discovered at Blickling) was erected by William I of the Norman line . . . as a residence for an Italian of remarkable wit and humour, who used by his sallies to enliven the dull, gloomy disposition of his barbarous court.'[18] This charming nonsense continues for two pages in which he enlarges on the possibility that the Italian was the ancestor of all the 18th-century pierrots and harlequins, but what it refers to is unclear; possibly the 'Madman's Tower' was an early idea for the crenellated Gothick folly next to the racecourse in the western part of the park, which was fitted out in the early 1770s.

The 2nd Earl's earliest alterations at Blickling were probably made in the early 1760s, when the Jacobean withdrawing chamber was divided into the Chinese Bedroom and its Dressing Room, both noticeably more rococo in character than the later alterations planned in 1765 after his diplomatic mission to Russia.

In August 1762 he was posted to St Petersburg as Ambassador at the Court of Catherine the Great. Horace Walpole's unkind characterisation of the youthful Buckinghamshire as 'the clearcake; fat, fair, sweet and seen through in a moment' describes adolescent qualities that developed in maturity into the good looks and amiable manners which it was hoped would please the Russian Empress. He attributed his failure to conclude the alliance between England and Russia in 1764 to the Treasury's meanness with resources, but socially he was a success. His letters to Lady Suffolk from St Petersburg[19] describe the Russian Court and its unfamiliar customs, the beauty of the Empress and her feats as a horsewoman. Buckinghamshire was particularly intrigued by the elaborate ceremonial of Court weddings and the contrasting informality of the balls, where all ranks and ages danced polonaises together, from 13-year-old maids of honour to octogenarian generals. Such entertainments were welcome diversions for an ambassador whose official duties were by no means onerous. His appearances at Court were occasional and the subject of special mention, but for the 18th-century correspondent the most spectacular event in Russia was the weather; the river in St Petersburg, the scene of summer barge races, was converted by the onslaught of November into 'a Broad Street' which on Sundays was 'covered with thousands of people who resort there to see sledge races and Boxing Matches'. Buckinghamshire actually preferred the depth of winter which provided 'excellent roads and a clear air which sharpens the appetite and enlivens the animals spirits' to 'the very concise summer of St Petersburg' when the vegetation came alive with a 'magick celerity' that recalled a childhood memory of 'an ingenious artist, who produced a tree which

blossomed, bore fruit and withered in less than ten minutes'. These extremes proved too much for his brother George who served as secretary and for whom one Russian winter was more than enough. In April 1763 Buckinghamshire wrote to tell Lady Suffolk that George was on his way home: 'At this moment he embraces his wife in thought and gallops an imaginary horse upon a visionary England'. His replacement was to be a source of considerable irritation but in other ways over the next year Buckinghamshire's posting became increasingly congenial, especially the languorous sunny mornings spent writing in the gardens of the Summer Palace whose 'shady walks, marble statues and fountains innumerable' he found pleasingly old-fashioned: 'Distant thunder, dark clouds, and screaming Peacocks pre-

The Chinese
Bedroom

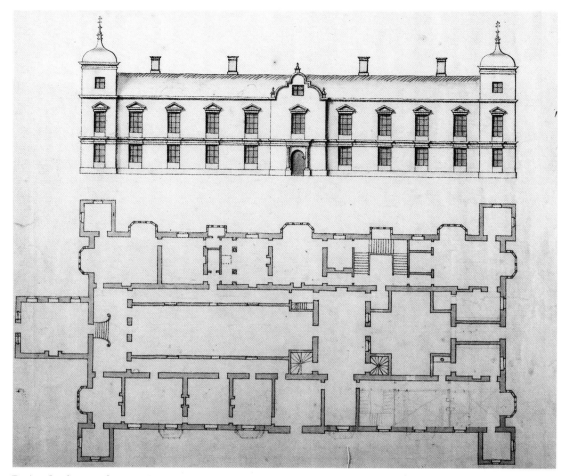

Design for the west front, mid-18th century

pare me to expect a storm, but I shall write on in perfect tranquillity til the first drops reach me. Whether it is a change of temper, or the effect of advancing further in life, I know not but I every day find that I contemplate every kind of storm with increasing tranquillity.'

This philosophical mood was brought to an end by the autumn of 1764 and his recall to England, where political events in Norfolk were not developing as he might have wished. His return became the subject of gloomy foreboding. 'My Norfolk history sits heaviest upon me,' he told his aunt, 'and the thought that I must never expect to pass a cheerful day at Blickling.'

In the event, however, local relationships were patched up and in 1765 Buckinghamshire embarked on a programme of repair and modernisation which was to

Design for the north front, William Ivory, 1765

occupy many happy years at Blickling. His architects were Thomas Ivory, who had worked as a carpenter in the 1st Earl's redecoration of the Long Gallery, and his son William. When the earliest plans for the 18th-century remodelling of Blickling were prepared is uncertain. The drawings of the 2nd Earl's alterations were made in 1765 and somewhat amended and supplemented in 1767. But there are earlier designs which could have been made around 1760. These early plans show the remodelling of the west front with a central neo-Jacobean gable and sash windows throughout, with alternative schemes for the recasting of the north front. In all cases the elevations show the towers reduced in height to something more like the scheme followed by many Palladian tower houses of the 18th century – Holkham (1732) and Kimberley (1763) are two local examples – whereas the later designs retained them at full height. The importance of these early drawings is

that they indicate an attempt to reflect the Jacobean character of the house; they are forerunners of the 2nd Earl's final scheme which was in itself one of the earliest instances of Jacobean revival.[20]

The 2nd Earl's work was planned in close consultation with his aunt. 'Nothing is more amusing' he wrote to her in November 1765, 'than to see numbers of workmen within and without doors: it is not exactly the same thing to pay their bills . . . Lady Buckinghamshire [Mary Ann Drury, his first wife] and Lady Dorothy [his sister] have entered into a conspiracy against the old chimney piece in the eating-room. Their little intrigues can never shake my settled purpose, but they tease me and your authority is necessary to silence them.' It is obvious that these words were not written with an entirely straight face, like another letter about the same room written later in that month, 'Gothic it was, and more Gothic it will be, in spite of all the remonstrances

The Great Hall by J. C. Buckler, 1820

of modern improvers and lovers of Grecian architecture. The ceiling is to be painted with the loves of Cupid and Psyche. Cupid is to hover exactly over the centre of the table, to indicate to the maître d'hôtel the exact position of the venison pasty'. By December, however, the fireplace joke had been pushed slightly too far and Lord Buckinghamshire warned his aunt of the ladies' intention to burn the venerable timbers in his absence. 'Let them at their peril,' he wrote, 'for you will resent it as well as I.'

Buckinghamshire also let Lady Suffolk have news of the radical changes that were proposed for the Great Hall in this year: 'I have determined what is to be done with the Hall which you ought to approve, and indeed must approve. Some tributory sorrow should be paid to the nine worthies; but Hector has lost his spear and his nose, David his harp, Godfrey of Boulogne his ears, Alexander the Great his highest shoulder, and part of Joshua's belly is fallen in. As the ceiling is to be raised eight of them must have gone, and Hector is at all

events determined to leave his niche.' He goes on to name eight 'worthies' of his own time, politicians whose 'figures are not as yet essentially mutilated', as possible replacements and suggests that 'as Anne Boleyn was born at Blickling, it will not be improper to purchase her father [sic] Henry the Eighth's figure (which by order is no longer to be exhibited at the Tower) who will fill with credit the space occupied by the falling Hector'.[21]

This valuable description of the Jacobean decoration in the Great Hall also shows that even though the 'eight worthies' project was not a serious one, the reliefs in niches of Queen Elizabeth and Anne Boleyn originated in the ancient scheme. In 1767 they were placed above the landings of a great double-flight staircase to which the Great Hall was now given over. It incorporated nearly all the timbers of the old Jacobean staircase, removed from the original site in the east front. The Ivorys' efforts to match the old timbers in softwood were more than adequate and in places it is quite difficult

The Lower Ante Room (Drinking Room), William Ivory, 1767

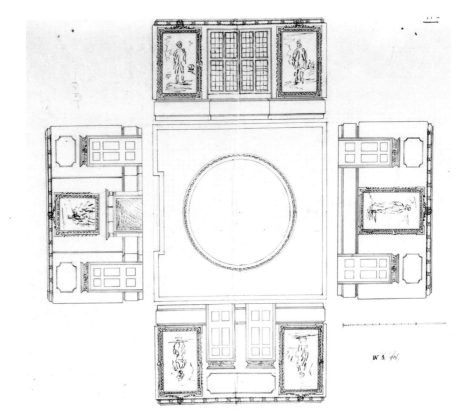

(Opposite page) Tapestry of Peter the Great at the Battle of Poltawa, woven in 1764

36

to distinguish their work from that of the Jacobean craftsmen. Some of their newel figures, however, are distinctly and deliberately modern (page 77). To make a decent approach to the stair foot and allow room for a gallery to communicate between the east and west ranges, the front wall of the Great Hall was demolished and rebuilt so that it stood proud of the flanking turrets.

The removal of the Jacobean staircase allowed the creation of a comfortable suite of rooms on the ground floor of the east front. A floor was introduced in the stairwell to create a 'Drinking Room' (the present Lower Ante Room) and on the first floor a tapestried ante-chamber to the Long Gallery and Drawing Room. The ground floor rooms to the north were Lady Buckinghamshire's dressing room and bed chamber (taking in the present Brown Room) and the 'Tool Closet'. Car-

Caroline Conolly, Countess of Buckinghamshire, by Thomas Gainsborough

pentry was evidently a hobby of his Lordship's and the inventory of 1793 reverentially records the single product of his pleasurable labours, 'My Lord's Paddle'. Further along the corridor was the 'Physic closet' which in 1793 contained an apparatus 'for Electrifying'; the use of mild shocks from static electricity was one of the health fads of the late 18th century. At the end was Lord Buckinghamshire's study with windows facing east and north.[22] In 1773 a staircase was installed in the adjacent turret to connect the study with the Library in the Long Gallery above.[23]

As work proceeded on the great staircase the medieval west range was being refronted and extensively re-modelled. William Ivory's design for this elevation was one of the least successful aspects of Lord Buckinghamshire's work. It had a completely straight parapet and, as its only concession to the Jacobean ranges, there were mullioned windows. It must have been this part of the building that prompted Silas Neville, who saw Blickling in 1782, to remark that 'The new part is very inferior and looks more like an hospital than a nobleman's seat'.[24] Lady Suffolk's death in 1767 was rapidly followed by that of the young Lady Buckinghamshire in 1769, and an inscription in the centre of the new west front records that her jewels were bequeathed to pay for its completion.

In 1770 Buckinghamshire married his second wife, Caroline, daughter of Sir William Conolly of Stratton Hall, Staffordshire. Visitors to Blickling at this time were not always made to feel welcome. Lady Beauchamp Proctor of Langley called with a party in September 1772 on her second tour of the Norfolk houses. 'We were afraid of being too soon, but on sending in our names were admitted. We found they had break-fasted, and my Lord's horses stood at the door, though the servant told us he was gone out. We saw no other traces of her Ladyship than two or three workbags and a tambour; I believe we drove her from room to room, but that we could not help. We saw only the old part of the house, over which a very dirty housemaid with a duster in her hand conducted us.' Just as the party was preparing to leave, Lord Buckinghamshire appeared and 'made a thousand courtier-like speeches, but they were so little worth attending to that they were in at one ear and out at t'other; one thing however I could not help remarking – he said he was mortified beyond expression that he happened to be out when we came, and you

The arms of
George II on the
bed in the State
Bedroom

know I have mentioned his horses being at the door when we came in'.[25]

In 1777 Lord Buckinghamshire became Lord Lieutenant of Ireland. It was an uncomfortable appointment, compromised by his relationship to the Conolly family – his brother-in-law, Thomas Conolly of Castletown, was one of the most vocal members of the Irish Parliament – and, despite the passage of several useful reforms, it was, by common consent, a failure. With relief he was able to return to England late in 1780, describing himself as 'a man whose mind has been ul-

cerated with a variety of embarrassments for thirty weary months'. In his absence, Thomas and William Ivory had been pushing ahead with the completion of the north front, whose overall design, set out in William Ivory's drawing of 1765, was finalised in 1768 when it was decided to have a flat lead roof, a stone balustrade and pedimented windows. It is an outstanding example of 'keeping in keeping' and even the texture and bond of the brickwork is virtually indistinguishable from the Jacobean work. The ground floor rooms here were well advanced by the time that the west wing was being fitted out in 1773 and the principal apartment at this level was the Organ Chamber. Strongly antiquarian in character, its doors and ceiling were decorated with small swirls of Gothick tracery.[26]. The medieval angels from Caister Castle, bought from the sale of Oxnead in 1732, were incorporated into the fireplace (removed to the Brown Room in 1858).

By November 1778 John Ivory, the marble mason, was being paid 100 guineas for a Sienna marble fireplace for the 'great room', now known as the Peter the Great Room, occupying the three central bays of the first floor.[27] The Peter the Great Room and its adjoining State Bedroom are the two most important 18th-century rooms at Blickling. They were conceived as a setting for the works of art which commemorated the high point of Buckinghamshire's career when he was Ambassador at St Petersburg; the spectacular tapestry of Peter the Great at the Battle of Poltawa presented to him by Catherine the Great in 1764, as well as the two portraits of George III and Queen Charlotte and the rich canopy of state which had accompanied his diplomatic mission (page 90).

In April 1779 Thomas Ivory was badly injured when his leg was crushed by a piece of timber and by late May his health was in 'a Dangerous and alarming state with strong symptoms of a mortification'. Unable to stir from his bed he would naturally have hoped that his son William would take over the work. But the country was now involved in a colonial war with France and, with the threat of invasion, militia companies were drilling all over England. Captain William Ivory, who could not be released from the manoeuvres of Sir John Wodehouse's militia at Coxheath camp, suggested that 'Mr Wyat' at London might undertake the carpenter's work for the alterations at the family's London house.[28]

Samuel Wyatt was then practising as architect, builder and timber merchant at Berwick Street, Soho. He was one of the leading exponents of 18th-century neo-classicism and by May 1780 was already directing alterations at the Buckinghamshires' Bond Street house.[29] The architecture of the State Bedroom at Blickling is so remarkably self-assured that it is hard to believe that the Ivorys, who had obvious difficulty assimilating new neo-classical ideas in the Peter the Great Room, were responsible for it. Samuel Wyatt may have designed this beautiful room through the basic plan, which is exactly similar to Lady Suffolk's bed chamber at Marble Hill, is that of William Ivory who early in 1779 submitted designs adapted 'in some measure to the stile of the House'. The decoration and furnishings here and in the Peter the Great Room were being completed in 1782.

It is possible to follow Lord Buckinghamshire's work at Blickling in such detail partly through correspondence with his conscientious but not always tactful agent, Robert Copeman. Opposed to the introduction of Wyatt, he wrote on the subject of the new Orangery in March 1781, 'Your Lordship having already built so much, I do not conceive what you can possibly build more, of any great Account and am therefore glad to find that this affair is so settled between your Lordship and her Ladyship that Mr Ivory may be consulted as to the plan of the Greenhouse rather than any new comer'.[30] But Lord Buckinghamshire had evidently changed his mind once more, for the new Orangery strongly recalls Wyatt's vine house at Holkham in its reserved use of Coade stone plaques and its marvellously delicate fanlights. Ivory's design for an orangery with Gothick windows and a large blind upper storey is dull by comparison and must have prompted this change of heart.

Relations between Copeman and Lord Buckinghamshire were often strained and did not improve as they grew older. Buckinghamshire was impatient and irascible and there were subjects which Copeman knew it was unwise to broach. On one occasion in 1791, when he had to report that the hothouse in the kitchen garden had burnt down, he wrote to Lady Buckinghamshire about it, having recently 'received a reprimand from his Lordship for giving him some unwelcome news in an evening'. For his part, however, Copeman could never resist volunteering his opinion when it was not required. On Lord Buckinghamshire's scheme to remove a columnar eye catcher in the garden (page 56) he inquired in January 1790, 'When such a seat is built do you think that your Lordship shall like the appearance of it? Is there any pleasant object to be seen from the seat when so placed and if your Lordship is disposed to walk must you not leave a pleasanter to go there?'. Buckinghamshire's reply is not known but Copeman's next letter begins characteristically, 'If I have offended your Lordship in any way I am very sorry for it and am as innocent of the cause as them who never saw or heard of your Lordship'.[31]

Having essentially completed the restoration of the house, the closing decade of Lord Buckinghamshire's life was spent in making adjustments. Water closets were installed, probably for the first time, in 1791[32] and small changes were made in the garden. Copeman's letter book of 1789–92 and the 2nd Earl's letters to his youngest daughter, Amelia, addressed as 'Dear Baby', reveal glimpses of a quiet life at Blickling, when the excitement of balls at St Petersburg and the splendour of Irish State banquets were replaced by the pleasurable anticipation of the Aylsham Assembly, 'We are very cheerful in our solitude,' he wrote in the spring of 1790–1, but 'do not breakfast till half an hour after nine o'clock when Bell [possibly the gamekeeper referred to as 'the Bloody Bell' for his conscientious control of vermin] comes down with eyes ajar complaining of the Rheumatics. Caroline [his daughter] more active, walks before breakfast . . . Mrs Butler performs to admiration to please my pallet, there cannot be a better cook, but the poor woman has got the Yellows. Your mama's new walk is visited every day and forms a most agreeable communication . . . there are numberless hares sporting about the park and woods, and many new married partridges enjoying their Honeymoon.'[33]

In 1792, he secured Caroline's marriage with William Harbord, heir to his near neighbour, Lord Suffield of Gunton. The family came to stay that December, when Lord and Lady Suffield were please to be given a warm room above the kitchen in the west range. Lord Buckinghamshire was solicitous for his son-in-law's health. 'Mr Harbord's gout is so far better that he walked yesterday to the Greenhouse. Such an attack is very unpleasant circumstance so early in life, it indeed concerns me to think that neither he nor Caroline will every enjoy vigorous health.'[34]

Lord Buckinghamshire was himself a victim of this common 18th-century complaint and, according to Horace Walpole, his death in 1793 was brought about by thrusting an imflamed foot into a bucket of icy water. On the 2nd Earl's death the title passed to his brother George, while Blickling went to his second daughter Caroline. His eldest daughter, Harriet, had incurred her father's displeasure by marrying the Earl of Belmore, whom she divorced in 1791; two years later she married the Earl of Ancram, who was later to becoame 6th Marquis of Lothian. Caroline and her husband, who became Lord Suffield in 1810, were childless so that the succession passed to the Lothians on Lord Suffield's

The Orangery

death in 1821. Lady Suffield, however, lived on at Blickling until 1850.

Surprisingly little is known about the long tenure of Lady Suffield. She and her husband began resolutely enough by inviting the fashionable London architect Joseph Bonomi to design a striking pyramidal mausoleum for the 2nd Earl, but it was many years before anything of comparable interest was added to the house. Lord Buckinghamshire had indeed left little scope for further work except perhaps in furnishing, and it is evident that in the first quarter of the 19th century the austere rooms of the Georgian house were given some of the comforts of the Regency. But there is no sign of any purposeful remodelling and it was not until the late 1820s that Lady Suffield made her mark on the house. She was an enterprising gardener and had employed Humphry Repton and his eldest son John at Gunton. In the 1820s John Adey Repton also worked on the garden at Blickling and on some of the buildings of the estate (page 59). A prolific writer on antiquarian subjects, he made additions to the house that were more scholarly and correct than even the most literal Jacobean essays of the Ivorys. Repton submitted designs for the west front c.1821 and for the reconstruction of the central clock tower c.1828, both of which, with minor changes, were carried out. The linking arcades between the house and wings are also his and there are drawings for neo-Jacobean furniture, some of which remained at Blickling until the 1930s. He also provided drawings for the ornamentation of the parish church.

Blickling twice escaped destruction by fire during the early part of the 19th century. The first was in 1808: people came from Aylsham to fight the blaze and gratuities were distributed in the town afterwards.[35] The second broke out in April 1849, and was described by Lady Suffield's agent, Robert Parmeter, who wrote, 'Mr. C. Marsham, who fortunately was staying in the House, informs me that but for the courage of his own servant, the under Butler & principal Footman of Lady Suffield and Mr Wells the Innkeeper . . . who exposed themselves to the fire and smoke of the Room almost to suffocation until the Flames were extinguished . . . it would have been impossible to save the house.'[36]

Lady Suffield died in the following year, aged 83, and was buried at Gunton. At last the Lothian family, for whom Blickling had been destined since 1821, could take full possession of the house.

NOTES

1 R. W. Ketton-Cremer, *Norfolk Portraits*, pp. 16–18.

2 NNRO NRS 12049 27 A6.

3 Historical Manuscripts Commission, 1905, p. 131.

4 NNRO 768A (uncatalogued).

5 Ibid NRS 11126.

6 Ibid NRS 23489 Z 103.

7 Ibid NRS 16335 32C2, NRS 1600731 F9.

8 Historical Manuscripts Commission, 1905, p. 131.

9 R. W. Ketton-Cremer, *Norfolk Portraits*, pp. 58–68.

10 NNRO NRS 11129 25 E5.

11 Historical Manuscripts Commission, 1905, p. 143.

12 NNRO MC3/59 466 x 3.

13 J. L. Phibbs, Blickling Park Survey, p. 16.

14 D. E. Howell James, 'Matthew Brettingham's Account Book', *Norfolk Archaeology* XXXV, 1971.

15 Illustrated in *Architectural History*, Vol. 7, 1964, p. 44.

16 NNRO NRS 19373 42 A4.

17 NNRO MC3/252 468 x 4.

18 J. W. Croker, *Lady Suffolk's Letters*, 1824, Vol. II, p. 239.

19 These letters are printed in Historical Manuscripts Commission, 1905, pp. 170–91.

20 The other contemporary examples are James Essex's work at Madingley Hall, Cambridgeshire (1758), Burton Constable, Yorkshire (1760), Capability Brown's remodelling of Corsham Court, Wiltshire (1761), and the remodelling of Audley End, Essex (commenced in 1762).

21 J. W. Croker op. cit. pp.304–10.

22 NNRO MC3/338 477 x 8.

23 NNRO NRS/4625.

24 *The Diary of Silas Neville 1767–1788*, Ed. Basil Cozens-Hardy, 1950, p. 298.

25 R. W. Ketton-Cremer, *Norfolk Assembly*, pp. 193–94.

26 NNRO NRS 19180 33 E7. The more complicated plasterwork here was undertaken by Joseph Rose.

27 NNRO NRS 14630.

28 NNRO NRS 19180 33 E7.

29 NNRO NRS 14630.

30 NNRO NRS 14625.

31 These exchanges are recorded in Copeman's letter book NNRO MC3 365 477 x 19180 33 E7.

32 NNRO MC3 365 477 x.

33 NNRO MC3 285.

34 Ibid.

35 NNRO MC3/61(a) 466 x 3.

36 NNRO NRS 18278 33 B1.

CHAPTER FOUR

BLICKLING UNDER THE LOTHIANS

William Schomberg Robert Kerr was nine years old when he became 8th Marquis of Lothian, and eighteen when he inherited Blickling. On his father's side his forebears were a Scottish border family whose titles included the barony of Jedburgh and the earldom of Ancrum; his mother was a Talbot. At Oxford he moved mostly in Catholic and High Anglican circles, no doubt influenced by his mother's earlier conversion to Catholicism. At Oxford, too, he met the architect William Butterfield and the inventive and adventurous decorative painter and architect John Hungerford Pollen.

In 1854 Lord Lothian married his first cousin, Lady Constance Talbot. Among the couple's friends in London were more notable artists; G. F. Watts was to

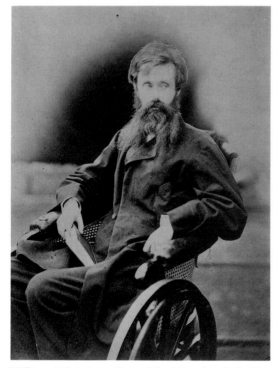

William Schomberg Kerr, 8th Marquis of Lothian (1832–70)

become the confidant of Lady Lothian, and her husband's early diaries record musical evenings at the home of Val Prinsep.

During the early years of their marriage the Lothians frequently travelled to France and Italy and in 1854 they had spent many months in India, chiefly in the north and in Tibet.[1] Early photographs of Blickling show how the rooms were furnished with their purchases. The family owned a large number of other houses, including Newbattle Abbey in Lothian, a huge and rambling mansion incorporating monastic remains, and the border castle of Ferniehurst. In the 1850s and 1860s the couple were constantly on the move; staying at Scottish fishing lodges, with the Talbots at Ingestre, the Salisburys at Hatfield and at their own London house in Upper Grosvenor Street.

Lady Suffield's agent, Robert Parmeter, was still in charge at Blickling. He was on much better terms with the young Lord Lothian than his predecessor and former partner Copeman had been with Lord Buckinghamshire, and the few letters from Lothian, some written during boring moments in debates in the House of Lords, are friendly and conversational.

Before departing for his travels in Asia, Lothian made arrangements for a memorial window to Lady Suffield at Blickling church. It was the collaborative effort of Butterfield and John Hardman whose stained glass, the first to recover the strength and purity of medieval painting, Lothian had admired in some of the newly built High Anglican churches in London. The Blickling window was a masterpiece of clear delineation and brilliant, jewel-like colour. The hurried visits of the busy architect are recorded by Robert Parmeter[2] who was disappointed when he would not stop for lunch and bemused when, notwithstanding the rector's polite complaints about the cold, the installation of the glass was delayed until the spring of 1856 by its display at an exhibition in Paris.[3]

After their return to England in 1856 the renovation

of Blickling became a major preoccupation for the Lothians. The division and enlargement of some of Lord Buckinghamshire's ground floor rooms on the east front was the first job and by 4 December 1857 the house was 'in all the confusion and *desolation* of Brick-layers and carpenters'[4] who were busy forming a new morning room (the present Brown Drawing Room). The architect of this work was Benjamin Woodward. the designer of the Debating Hall at the Oxford Union built in 1857, where Pollen, Morris, Burne-Jones, Rossetti, Val Prinsep and others worked together on the spectacular but now much-faded mural decoration. In the following year Pollen had joined Woodward at Blickling,[5] devising for the morning room a wonderful beamed ceiling decorated with entwined birds and serpents painted on strips of canvas. This highly original decoration survives above a later suspended ceiling and is recorded in drawings and photographs.

Just as remarkable in its way was the ceiling of Lady Lothian's sitting room at the north end of the east front,

Detail of the east window of Blickling church by John Hardman, 1856

Lady Constance Talbot, Marchioness of Lothian (1836–1901), by John Leslie

in which Pollen painted broad bands of Celtic interlace over a sky of wheeling birds; it has long since been painted over. In the Long Gallery, however, much of his decoration remains. The work here coincided with the construction of the University Museum in Oxford where Woodward worked with Pollen and two gifted Irish sculptors, the brothers O'Shea. Lord Lothian, a generous contributor to the Museum Sculpture Fund, was able to involve this team at Blickling. By 1858 the books had been removed from the room and in the following year carpenters were recasting the 1st Earl's presses into their new powerful Gothic profile, and John O'Shea began to carve their uprights into naturalistic foliage[6], inspired no doubt by local trees and plants, just as specimens from Oxford's Botanical Gardens had been lovingly copied for the Museum. A huge hooded marble chimney-piece arrived in 1860;[7] Gothic in overall form, it was carved to Pollen's design with strange birds, Islamic patterns and, in the centre, two Hobart bulls carved in low relief and affronted like the figures in the Lion Gate at Mycenae, beneath a tree hung with heraldry. The fireplace has gone but the extraordinary eclecticism of its decoration is recalled by the painted frieze around the upper walls of the gallery. Here Renaissance white vine interlace – inspired perhaps by the 15th-century Suetonius manuscript which is one of the greatest treasures of the Blickling library – coils round figures of art and literature before a strongly rendered Khelim backcloth. Curtains of woven strips, decorated with Pollen's designs, were made in Algeria.

O'Shea, who had not been able to complete his work at the Museum through lack of funds, was equally unlucky at Blickling and in February 1861 Parmeter wrote to express his concern that the estate was running out of money and advocating economies.[8] The carving and

some of Pollen's painted decoration was left unfinished, but the rest of the project was completed by 1863.

Pollen had particularly relished the experience of working at Blickling and wrote to his wife in May 1860: 'As you know, a great green pleasure-ground of 20 acres stretches on the south [*sic*] of this house, and is bounded by a huge grove of the noblest oak and beech. All day long this paradise has been full of the chuckling of suppressed delight from innumerable jovial dicky-birds, sitting and guggling away with their own fun; a sort of bursting up of the fountains of life and joy . . . . The keeper brought me a Jackdaw, a starling, a white owl, a gossander, a widgeon; I caught a little swallow during the hurricane, when in their terror they crouched down on the ground in flocks . . . and at night a goat-sucker flew round me in a stealthy way. . . .'[9] Many of

Lisa, a scene from Boccaccio's *Decameron* by Val Prinsep, in the 'O' Bedroom

Blickling's birds and animals found their way into his decoration in the Long Gallery.

Lord Lothian had gradually instituted improvements to make Blickling a more comfortable house. The waterworks were reorganised in 1857,[10] gas was introduced in the following year[11] and in 1862 Haden & Jones of Trowbridge had installed a 'warming apparatus' whose grills are still visible.[12] The bedrooms of the west front had been redecorated and refurnished; each known by a letter of the word Lothian in imitation of the 18th-century Buckingham Row on the top floor. Now William Burn, the aged and highly respected country house architect who had done so much to establish the neo-Jacobean style and who had worked at Newbattle in 1836, was called in to devise improvements to the domestic offices and other areas.

Burn's job was to plan a new range of offices in the west wing and provide servants' accommodation.[13] The west wing was completely rebuilt, retaining only its Jacobean front wall. Parmeter described this hair-raising building operation in a letter to Lord Lothian in September 1864, discussing the necessity of taking down the north-east gable: 'It is a marvel to see how the others stand deprived of their roof and back walls. They

(*Above*) Detail of J. H. Pollen's painted decoration in the Long Gallery

(*Left*) The Brown Drawing Room

weathered, however, a very high wind that we had last Friday and are supported by a great amount of scaffolding.'[14] The raising of its rear wall enabled the rebuilt wing to accommodate a new kitchen, laundry, brewhouse and game larders. Burn had hoped to build accommodation for servants in a structure that would have joined this wing to the house but Lord Lothian was emphatic that Blickling's appearance should not be spoilt by this addition, and the accommodation was squeezed into the lower floors of the west front. In the course of the work, Burn was dismayed to discover that the 9-inch brick facing with which the Ivorys and then John Repton had encased the ancient west front 'had been carried up without a single bond stone or brick being introduced into the old wall'.[15] But in the end he was able to retain most of the Georgian work, inserting the necessary bonds with such skill that there is now no obvious sign of the crisis.

But the 8th Marquis was not long to enjoy these im-

Philip Kerr, 11th Marquis of Lothian (1882–1940)

The Great Hall as decorated by the 8th Marquis

provements and in 1870, at the age of 38, he finally succumbed to the disease which he is thought to have contracted in India and which had latterly confined him to a wheelchair. Eight years later, G. F. Watts carved for the church a stupendous effigy of veined alabaster, attended by life-sized angels. Lady Lothian's restoration of the church, undertaken in two phases, in 1872 and 1876,[16] was also a memorial to her husband, and for the first time since perhaps the 17th century the tower was raised to a height that allowed the church to make its presence felt in a village that had hitherto been completely dominated by the house, a practical demonstration of the power of Victorian piety. The principal consolation of Lady Lothian's long widowhood, however, was the development of the gardens at Blickling (page 59).

From Lady Lothian's death in 1901, Blickling was let to tenants until 1932 when Philip Kerr, 11th Marquis of Lothian, decided to make the house his principal English seat.

Kerr, who had somewhat reluctantly inherited his title two years earlier, was a man of vision and ability who was to play a crucial part in the international diplomacy of the Second World War before his premature death in 1940. A convinced Liberal, he became private secretary to Lloyd George in 1916 and drafted the preface to the Treaty of Versailles in 1919. He resigned in 1921 to devote more time to journalism and travel in his capacity as Secretary of the Rhodes Trustees. In 1931, when he joined the all-party Cabinet of Ramsay MacDonald, he was made Chancellor of the Duchy of Lancaster and, a few months later, Under Secretary of State for India. He resigned from the administration in 1932 when he found its policies incompatible with his strong belief in Free Trade. It was at this time that he turned his attention to Blickling, which he saw as a quiet place for writing and for gatherings of politicians and academics; especially the meetings of *The Round Table*, an influential quarterly journal devoted to Im-

perial and Commonwealth politics, of which he had been the founding editor in 1910.

Lothian was an idealist and something of an eccentric. His friends despaired of his untidy appearance which was redeemed by boyish good looks and a lack of self-consciousness typified by his arrival at Westminster Abbey for the coronation of George VI in an Austin 7. Some of his earliest visits to Blickling were made on a much-loved motorcycle.

After years of letting Lothian found the house gloomy and drab; its rooms, cluttered with Victorian furniture whose arrangement had been muddled by successive tenants, in a state of unattractive decay.

It took 33 workmen 14 months to bring Blickling up to date to serve the needs of Lord Lothian and his distinguished guests. The Great Hall was painted white, its stained glass and many of the full-length portraits were removed and stored. Elsewhere in the house much of the powerful and idiosyncratic high Victorian decoration was painted out or otherwise concealed; Sheraton and Chippendale furniture was bought to replace the Victorian pieces. Lothian appears to have been influenced by Christopher Hussey's articles in *Country Life* in 1930 which directed specific criticism at the fireplace in the Long Gallery and the elaborate Parterre of Lady

The South Drawing Room in the early 20th century

Lothian. With hindsight the destruction of the fireplace was very regrettable, but the transformation of the Parterre and the simplification of the Victorian planting in the Temple Walk was an inspired piece of gardening (page 60).

Lord Lothian only stayed at Blickling for short periods, but this was the last time the Hall operated on a full scale. The establishment of 12 resident domestic servants was equivalent to the Victorian complement and the only significant changes were the abandonment of the laundry in the west wing and the employment of fewer gardeners. On some weekends there were 36 fires for the housemaids to tend and on still autumn afternoons a pall of smoke would hang over the house. At Round Table 'moots' Lord Halifax, Sir Edward Grigg, Lionel Curtis and Lord and Lady Astor would congregate at an oak table in the South Drawing Room for meetings which often included foreign diplomats and men of affairs from the Commonwealth.[17]

Although he had no taste for shooting, Lothian allowed the Astors' sons to do so. On the occasions when their parents accompanied them Nancy Astor would lower the blinds in order not to witness the carnage, and there was an atmosphere of restraint, but on other weekends the housemaids would have to clear up the debris of cut-flower fights and bath salt battles.

Lord Lothian's reputation as a statesman was somewhat tarnished by his association with the Cliveden set and their pro-German influence on British foreign policy in the run up to the Second World War. Von Ribbentrop, Berlin's ambassador at the Court of St James, stayed at Blickling in 1934 and left his arrogant signature in the visitors' book. But Lord Lothian, who had only ever supported liberal groups in pre-war Germany, was to play a leading part in defeating Hitler during the short period of his embassy at Washington in 1939–40. It was he who persuaded Churchill to write the historic letter to Roosevelt which for the first time gave the Americans an unequivocal statement of Britain's depleted military strength. At a daringly timed press conference in Washington, Lothian delivered a similar message to the American public, helping to create a political climate that allowed the President to give substantial assistance to the Allies. This was the culmination of months of travel and speeches by Lothian which, in stressing America's interest rather than the plight of the Allies, had helped to turn opinion across the United States. Tragically this punishing schedule took its toll of Lothian's health. Some years earlier, under the influence of Nancy Astor, he had become a Christian Scientist. Now his beliefs would not allow him to submit to medical treatment.

Just before one of his last trips to Washington, Lothian, standing at the window gazing out over the lake at Blickling, remarked to Miss O'Sullivan, his secretary, 'Now that it has come to the point, I don't want to go; I may never see this again'. Whether these words were prompted by the general insecurity of the times or some sense of his own impending death, is uncertain, but he saw Blickling only once more, in October 1940, when in a brief and busy visit to England he spent a day at the house which had since been requisitioned as the Officers' Mess for RAF Oulton. He ordered some of the soft furnishing which had been put away for safekeeping to be brought out to make the officers more comfortable. He returned to Washington in November 1940 and died of uremic poisoning on 12 December.

NOTES

1 This expedition is described in Lord Lothian's manuscript diaries, 1851–57, held at Blickling.

2 NNRO NRS 18278 33 B1.

3 NNRO NRS 18273 33 B1.

4 NNRO NRS 18274 33 B1.

5 NNRO MC3/141.

6 NNRO MC3/141.

7 NNRO NRS 18275 33 B1.

8 Ibid.

9 Anne Pollen, *John Hungerford Pollen*, 1912, f.284–5.

10 NNRO NRS 18274.

11 NNRO MC3/171 466 x 8.

12 NNRO MC3/169 466 x 7.

13 Burn's suggestion for a great saloon occupying the rear courtyard, and communicating with all the main rooms, was not taken up. Neither was the later idea for the extension of the great staircase through a central arch and up to a first-floor corridor, running the length of the Long Gallery. NNRO NRS 19373 42 A4.

14 NNRO NRS 18275 33 B1.

15 NNRO MC3/263/1.

16 NNRO MC3/536/2.

17 Information kindly given by Mrs Doris Skinner, one of Lord Lothian's housemaids.

CHAPTER FIVE

THE BOOKS

It is perhaps difficult to imagine a country house without a library, but it is almost certain that no provision would have been made for such a room in the Jacobean house with Lyminge built for Sir Henry Hobart at Blickling. Libraries were introduced into the layout of none of the great houses built before the Restoration: there was no library at Longleat, none at Hardwick, and none at Hatfield. At Blickling the tradition is unlikely to have been broken.

That is not to say that many men of the first rank socially did not own books. When they did, though, there is no evidence that they displayed them in any special room and on shelves as was, of course, the practice in college and cathedral libraries. In country houses books were generally stored in the traditional way – in trunks. When the great 'Wizard' Earl of Northumberland died at Petworth in 1632 his large collection was found in fifty: they were admittedly in what was called the 'Librarie', but it would not have been recognisable as such today.[1] We can be almost certain that Sir Henry Hobart would not have asked for a room to be fitted up in any new-fangled way to hold his books. He probably intended, on the other hand, to have had some volumes out on shelves in a study – a closet he would have called it – a room perhaps attached to his bedchamber. Such an arrangement is often found, but these closets were essentially private rooms, not great public ones as we imagine libraries.

We can only guess, too, about the books that Sir Henry owned, for none can now be identified. We can be sure that he had books: as a judge who rose to the top of his profession, he must have had at least a working library of law books, which he would have kept where they were of most use to him – in his chambers in London.

No books that belonged to succeeding generations of Hobarts have survived either: with their financial problems at the end of the 17th century, the family may have sold books along with their other possessions. In the mid 18th century, though, Blickling acquired what is still one of the most remarkable country-house libraries in England. In 1742 the 1st Earl's distant kinsman, Sir Richard Ellys of Nocton in Lincolnshire, died entailing most of his property on the death of his second wife on the Hobarts. Although Lady Ellys lived another 27 years, she remarried in 1745, and it was then that the great collection of books was brought to Blickling; certainly when Lord Buckinghamshire died in 1756 the valuation taken shows that he had spent more than £1,000 fitting up the Long Gallery – presumably to receive Ellys's books.

Poppies from Columna's *Icones*: the impression of the leaves is produced by pressing inked specimens. Early 17th century

Ellys is a surprisingly shadowy figure. The title was not an old one, his grandfather had been made a baronet by Charles II in 1660, but the family was clearly rich and of some social standing. It is odd, therefore, that the date of Sir Richard's birth is not known for certain: it is generally given as about 1674. He appears to have gone to neither Oxford nor Cambridge and it is said he was educated abroad, probably in the Low Countries. He sat in Parliament for Grantham from 1701 to 1705 and later represented Boston for 15 years from 1719. He is said as well to have been a Dissenter and a member of Calamy's congregation in London. Apart from the names of his two wives, neither of whom bore him any children, very little is known of his life. What is clear, though, is that he was a most remarkable, and famous, collector of books. He did not escape the attention of Horace Walpole, who called him 'a rich childless baronet . . . [who] pretended to learning on the credit of a very expensive library'.[2] Walpole is characteristically waspish, but his comment does contain some truth. Ellys certainly spent a great deal of money on his collection: in May 1732, for example, he owed Dieterik de Haan of Amsterdam the huge sum of £991 11s.[3] De Haan was presumably only one of many dealers he was using. Through his agents he was certainly active at many of the great sales of the 1720s and 1730s in England as well as on the Continent. Books surviving at Blickling show that he bought, for example, when Loménie de Brienne's books were sold in London in 1724, at Bridges's great sale in 1726, at Colbert's in Paris two years later, at the several Thomas Rawlinson sales from 1721 to 1733 and at Hearne's in 1736. A letter written from Holland only a few months before Ellys's death reports on the success in Vilenbourch's auction; the same letter shows he was getting ready to bid at the vast sales of Edward Harley, Earl of Oxford, though death was to prevent him.[4]

In his collecting Ellys relied heavily on the services of John Mitchell, who lived in his house in Bolton Street in London and acted as his librarian. He was largely responsible for the catalogue in manuscript now at Blickling; many of the books bear an 'M' on the free endpaper, showing he had examined them; many, too, bear a brief bibliographical note – that all the plates are indeed present, pointing out that a book is imperfect, or that leaves have been misbound – in his hand. It was to Mitchell that agents reported on the success of sales. He kept both a 'List of books subscribed for'[5] and anno-

tated it – 'I believe it will never be done' is typical; and 'A list of several things laid by me in drawers and elsewhere'.[6] There are as well copy letters of Ellys's in Mitchell's hand. He seems, in fact, to have acted as his secretary. Mitchell's role has hitherto been entirely overlooked and all his work attributed to Michael Maittaire, the classical scholar and author of the *Annales Typographici*, who it is known was patronised by other aristocratic collectors like Harley and Pembroke. Maittaire may have offered Ellys advice, as Dibdin asserts,[7] but letters by Mitchell which have survived in the British Library[8] prove beyond a doubt that the hand which wrote the catalogue and annotated the books was Mitchell's not Maittaire's; his is the 'M' not Maittaire's. Since Ellys was relying on Mitchell rather than on a scholar of international reputation like Maittaire, his role in the choice of books must have been greater than was thought, his intellectual stature more considerable than Walpole's 'pretended to learning' acknowledges.

Suetonius's *Lives of the Twelve Caesars*, 1452, showing the beginning of the life of Augustus with the arms of the Este family

The range and quality of the library shows anyway that if it was a pretence, it was a good one; so good, indeed, that it is difficult to characterise it briefly and begin to do it justice. Walpole's 'expensive' must intend far more than big money spent: not only are many of the books beautiful copies, beautifully bound, but many are scarce. Ellys's was a collector's collection.

Ellys's own particular academic interests were philological: he was especially interested in the text of the Bible and produced a study of certain words and phrases in the New Testament, *Fortuita Sacra*, published at Rotterdam in 1727. Not surprisingly, therefore, his collection contained many works on Greek and Latin as well as on oriental languages, including an important Greek lexicon of Joannes Caspar Suicerus in 11 manuscript volumes and a copy of Robert Estienne's *Thesaurus Linguae Latinae*, specially printed on large sheets so that the author could make revisions. The collection is rich, too, in versions and translations of the Bible including 16th-century polyglots, the great early Greek editions, three Latin Bibles printed before 1500,

two copies of Coverdale's version, and the 'Red Indian' Bible printed at Cambridge, Massachusetts, in 1661–63, as well as others in French, Italian, and Spanish; the Old and New Testaments are separately represented, as are particular books in many editions. Not surprisingly perhaps, Ellys also owned commentaries on the Bible and its text from the Greek and Latin Fathers to those of his contemporaries. Beyond these particular specialities, the collection is as balanced as any in a great country house sought to be: the works of the authors of Greece and Rome; the history of the ancient world, its topography and antiquities; travellers' tales; science and medicine; descriptions of the countries of Europe, their history and their literature; works of natural history and law; and, of course, the history and the antiquities, the politics and the governance, the laws and the customs of England. But it was what Ellys collected within these broad categories which raised his collection so far above the usual.

In his collecting Ellys was moved, as were other learned men at the time, by the same spirit which had led to the refounding of the Society of Antiquaries of

The Digest in seven volumes, Paris, 1527–33, each differently bound by Claude Picques

From a manuscript inventory of artillery pieces made in France and dated 1609

London, had led men to learn Anglo-Saxon, to excavate the sites of the remote past, to hang up 'medieval' achievements in their churches, to begin to write the great county histories. Ellys had a real eye for the old and the antique, for the rare and the curious; but he had an eye too for the beautiful. He bought, for example, almost a hundred books published before 1500: these productions of the early presses of Europe were becoming a collector's taste. Again amongst the discriminating were books produced by the Aldine Press at Venice: Ellys pursued these elegant octavos, acquiring a number at Bridges's sale in 1726. Several are in contemporary, or early, bindings. Ellys had an eye for bindings: there are four that belonged to Jean Grolier, including the only surviving book from his library bound in velvet over stiff boards; but others in similar taste from the first half of the 16th century include an octavo edition of the Digest in seven volumes, each of them differently bound by Claude Picques. These are beautiful, but would also undoubtedly have been regarded as 'curiosities'. Of home-grown products Ellys had a number which would have been regarded as 'curious' too: the Books of

Common Prayer of 1549 and 1552 and the Scotch book of 1637; 16th-century books in English, generally religious, like Hearne's copy of *The Last Wil and Last Confession of Martyn Luthers Faith*, 1543; and a notable and extensive collection of Civil War pamphlets.

Ellys lived too early to buy the great colour-plate books of the late 18th and early 19th centuries, but Blickling still contains remarkable books of engravings notable as much for their number as their quality. It contains as well a number of great atlases by Blaeu and a unique maritime one by Doncker of 1667. He had a set of the spectacular 'Cabinet du Roi' illustrating every aspect of the Sun King's life at Versailles – his buildings, his fountains, his tapestries. These were rich men's books. But the spectacular plate books were always supplemented by learned treatises, whether on horsemanship or shells, consumption or jewels; there are works on chocolate, imported mineral waters, experiments on vipers, and nervous diseases; he owned the catalogue of the library of Harvard College recording the collection before the disastrous fire of 1764, Maundsell's *The First Part of the Catalogue of English Books*, 1595, and a collection of masses by Karel Luyton printed at Prague in 1611.

Although Ellys made a considerable collection of con-

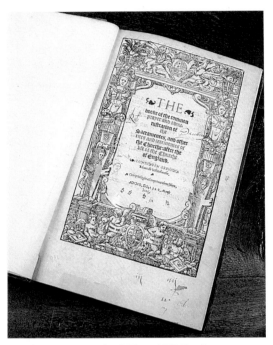

The first Prayer Book of Edward VI, London, 1549

Ellys's collection is remarkable for its range and depth, the results of his learning, his antiquarianism and his wealth. We do not know if he made it available to scholars in the way that Harley opened his library at Wimpole, but Walpole's remarks show that the library was well known; and it continued to be well known. Guides to Norfolk produced in the second half of the 18th century prove that the house was shown: none fails to mention the Long Gallery. It is, indeed, often recommended as the best room in the house, though its proportions (too long for its width, it was alleged) sometimes offended; in a subordinate clause the collection was generally praised. It is clear, though, that it was better known to the learned world: a number of Dibdin's extravagant and mannered outpourings refer to volumes in 'the magnificent old library at Blickling' (*The Library Companion*, 1824)[9] – the Sedan New Testament, the Book of Common Prayer of 1549, the Olivet Cicero 'in *uncut* state'.[10] Dibdin tells us too how the library was run: 'the interesting room is under the care of the Rev. Mr Churchill, librarian, and chaplain to the Dowager Lady Suffield'. 'I cannot refrain from indulging in one minute's delightful recollection,' he continues, 'of the morning, passed within its precincts, when, in company with Atticus, and Marcus, and Petronius, we revelled and rioted midst strange Greek MSS, and quaint printed tomes; a morning, followed up by a hospitable carousel at the Tusculum of Mr Churchill . . .'.[11] Dibdin was chiefly interested in bibliographical curiosities; Joseph Churchill, however, dealt with enquiries of a more academic kind. In about 1819 he received a letter

temporary political pamphlets and of occasional verse, the general absence of English literature is striking. Apparently he had no Chaucer, no Spenser, no Donne, no Herbert, most strange of all no Prior, a poet patronised, almost kept, by Harley; none of the Elizabethan and Jacobean dramatists – except Shakespeare, represented, however, by nothing but an octavo edition of 1735 – there was nothing of Marlowe or Jonson, Beaumont or Fletcher. Quartos of the early dramatists, so sought after by other collectors, would surely have been to his taste. The Restoration playwrights were also wanting. If he were a Puritan, it may have led him to disapprove of the stage.

At a time when some of his contemporaries, like Harley, were pursuing manuscripts so vigorously, he did not collect them in any serious way. Two dozen, though, have survived in the house, including a beautiful humanist Suetonius. Considering they were no particular interest of his it is perhaps strange that he should have owned both a Psalter of the 8th century and the great sermon collection, the Blickling Homilies, dated 971, two manuscripts of the very first importance. Both were sold by Lord Lothian in 1932.

The turtle from Mark Catesby's *The Natural History of Carolina, etc.*, London, 1731

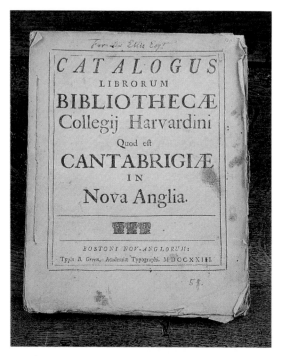

The first catalogue of the library at Harvard, presented to 'Mr' Ellis

Lady Suffield herself was a reader of novels, and first editions of *Emma*, *Pride and Prejudice*, and *Sense and Sensibility* are only the most well known of those still preserved in the house. What she is unlikely to have been able to do, however, is to have kept her books anywhere in the Long Gallery. Ellys's books filled it. Lack of space may have discouraged the Lothians from moving many of their family books to the house when they inherited it in 1850; the books at Blickling still remain principally Richard Ellys's collection.

It is remarkable for its quality; it is remarkable, too, that it has been preserved virtually intact. The libraries in many country houses were pillaged from the turn of the century, but chiefly between the wars. In 1932 Philip Kerr sold some 160 lots of books in New York: considering the state of the stock market, his timing was not impeccable. However much he regretted the sale its necessity was clear, raising more than £100,000: the money was paid straight to the Exchequer to settle death duties. The survival of Lord Lothian's estates was assured for another generation. Amongst those books consigned in 1932 were the 8th-century Psalter and the great Blickling Homilies. Most of the books he sold came, however, from another house, Newbattle Abbey. He might have sold many more from Blickling, but he did not. The collection is largely unscathed; it remains as Walpole said, 'a very expensive library'.

from the Rev. Robert Walpole asking him to look something up for him: 'I know your readiness always to work for me amongst the learned dead in Blickling Library';[12] he also asked that Churchill permit Mr Bloomfield of Cromer an hour or two in the Library. About the same time Edmund Henry Barker of Thetford, a Greek lexicographer of some note, wrote to say he had asked Lord Suffield to lend him two etymological manuscripts; Lord Suffield had said no; would he not waive his rule of lending nothing because of 'the national undertaking' on which Barker was engaged?[13] Churchill applied again to Lord Suffield, who found Barker's arguments did not induce him to 'break through the Rule of the Library'.[14] The correspondence continued throughout 1819 and 1820 with Churchill supplying readings from the manuscripts. These surviving examples of visitors coming to Blickling to see the books and of the questions put to Churchill are doubtless typical of many. The Suffields, moreover, were clearly quite well aware of the value of Ellys's library. A number of bibliographical reference works were added in the early 19th century, perhaps to help Churchill with his work.

NOTES

1 Syon MSS H. II. 1b.

2 In his edition of the poems of Sir Charles Hanbury Williams, London, 1822, v.1, pp.47–8.

3 B[odleian] L[ibrary] O[xford] MS D. D. Dashwood 12/3/4.

4 BLO MS D. D. Dashwood 12/3/17a.

5 BLO MS D. D. Dashwood 12/3/6.

6 BLO MS D. D. Dashwood 12/3/5.

7 *The Library Companion*, London, 1824, p. 578.

8 MS Add. 6210; see, for example, f. 92.

9 Ibid., p.30.

10 Ibid, pp.40, 43, 578.

11 P.578. Tusculum in this case was a villa at Cromer.

12 NNRO MC3/321 468 x 5.

13 NNRO MC3/320/1.

14 NNRO MC3/320/2.

CHAPTER SIX
THE GARDEN

The Norfolk climate is not a gentle one and, while it has never impeded the establishment of trees, it can be unkind to gardens. The luxuriant beauty of Blickling is therefore the achievement of inspired planting and carefully planned shelter. The garden today presents an impression of coherence that belies its history. Three centuries of good husbandry have made it one of England's great gardens and the contributions of Blickling's many owners underlie its serene unity.

Since the 17th century the main garden at Blickling has been on the east side of the house. Robert Lyminge certainly had a hand in the first layout, and the annotations on his drawing for a 'banketting house' (page 24) betray important clues about the overall design of Sir Henry Hobart's vanished garden. The wall in which this covered seat was set faced the house, on a terrace or 'high walk' which was clearly parallel with the east front. It would have formed one side of a formal garden whose centrepiece was perhaps a white marble fountain for which Thomas Larger was handsomely paid in 1620.[1] The 'banketting house' drawing also makes clear that the 'high walk' led north to a wilderness, which was no doubt a second rectangular enclosure containing a geometrical layout of walks and hedges. The large square of water which once lay before the north front was known in the late 17th century as the 'Wilderness Pond', presumably because it formed one side of this wilderness. Two further features may have defined the central axis of the Jacobean garden. One was a dovehouse which the survey commissioned in 1729 illustrates at the garden's southern extremity, and the other may be an early mount, largely demolished in 1688–89, whose remains could be indicated by the curving brick Victorian bastion to the north of the present Parterre. This strong north/south axis explains something about the design of the Jacobean east front and its asymmetrically placed garden door; this was an elevation to be viewed diagonally and not frontally as it is seen today.

The late 17th-century Hobarts seem to have made

their own contribution to the old layout before the entire scheme was swept away,[2] a transformation made clear by an ostentatious survey map, decorated with the recently acquired Order of the Bath, which the future 1st Earl of Buckinghamshire commissioned from James Corbridge in 1729. It shows that in the early 18th century the whole garden was turned through 180 degrees to achieve a more expansive if less intricate plan, in which the most powerful axis now ran from west to east, from the house to the temple.

These great new pleasure grounds probably extended north and involved the building of the new mount. They incorporated the old square Wilderness Pond, creating a new and complex woodland area, laid out on a grid of intersecting paths at the eastern boundary of the park. A huge terrace was thrown up here to complete the design and provide views to the more distant landscape, while the Doric temple which stood in the midst of this great earthwork dominated a new and imposing vista that ran down to the house.

The geometrical woodland layout in its original form did not survive long; in the 1760s it was planted up by the 2nd Earl[3] who created an informal network of meandering paths that reflected his alterations to the wider landscape of the park (see Chapter 7). The principal flower garden at this time was an oblong enclosure made out of the northern portion of the woodland area. It was the domain of Lady Buckinghamshire and in 1765 contained 'the greatest profusion of Minionet Roses, mirtles and honeysuckles'. Some of the 1st Earl's garden ornaments had been purchased from the sale of Oxnead in 1732 – the statue of Hercules, now in the Orangery, and the fountain placed in the centre of the Parterre – and in the same way the 2nd Earl in 1787 bought a screen of columns from the demolition of nearby Irmingland Hall.[4] At various points in the garden the Buckinghamshires placed 'seats', white painted timber shelters with tarred roofs and backs. But the most important garden building of the late 18th century

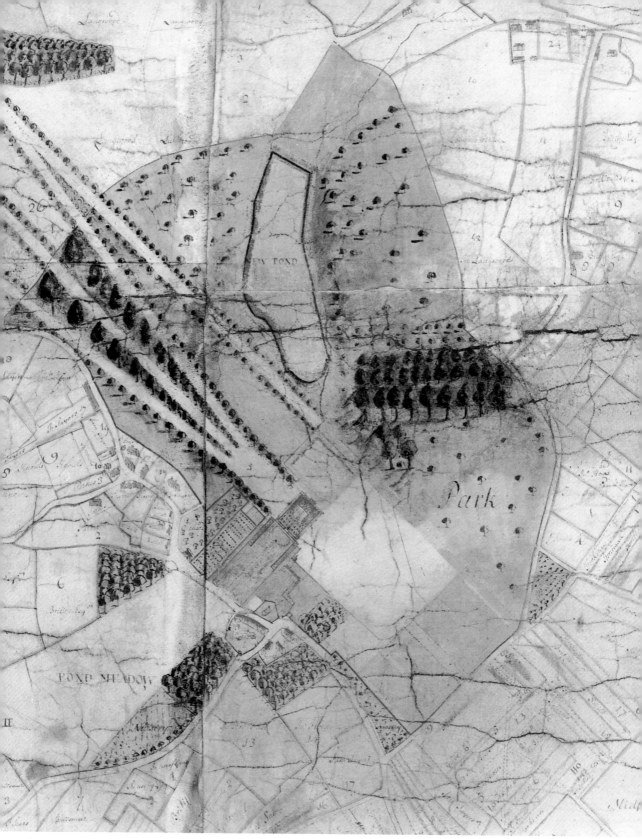

James Corbridge's survey of the park in 1729

was the Orangery, built in 1782 on the southern boundary of the garden and overlooking what has been known ever since as Greenhouse Park.

Humphry Repton often stayed with his sister Dorothy Adey in Aylsham and in an undated letter to her of *c*.1800 he suggested improvements to the garden at Blickling. 'You may perhaps like to explain [them] to Lady Suffield as your own idea,' he wrote, 'for I know by experience that the opinion of a professional man is only valuable in proportion as it is paid for – but you will recollect when I saw the flower garden at Blickling – I said it would be possible to enlarge it without destroying the beautiful holly hedge', which Repton goes on to advocate should be clipped into the '*Proscenium* to a fine *Amphitheatre* . . . surrounded by a clipt hedge over which the fine wood will appear like a scene in one of Watteau's paintings'.[5]

In 1816 the designs that Repton's son, John, was producing for Gunton included an orangery, the plans for which are preserved at Blickling along with a number of Repton schemes which may refer to either property.

(*Above*) Rough sketch by John Adey Repton for a circular planter

(*Right*) Design by John Adey Repton for a rustic temple

The Parterre *c*.1920

Lady Suffield certainly employed John extensively at Blickling after 1823. Many of the drawings are extremely rapid sketches which, for the younger Repton, completely deaf from birth, must have been an essential means of communication with his client. Perhaps some of them are hers. They include designs for trellises, pedestals, alcove seats, a charming little temple built of rustic poles, its pediment crested and swagged with fir cones, and a design dated 1823 for a Hardenburg basket which Repton first designed for Prince Hardenburg's seat at Potsdam in 1821–22. Several drawings are similar in their details to the trellis seat which still stands in the Secret Garden.

It is unlikely that Lady Suffield's extensive work did more than reinforce the informal framework developed by the 2nd Earl and it was left to her successors, the Lothians, to bring the evolution of the gardens full circle by resurrecting some of the 1st Earl's geometric planting designs. The first stage of this work was accomplished in 1863–64.[6] The margin of the lake was pushed back, new terraces made, old ones reshaped and enlarged, and a simplified version of the intersected walks indicated by the Corbridge survey laid out and planted up.

This return to formality is characteristic of country-house gardening after 1840. But the revival of the 18th-century woodland design at Blickling was an unusual and most successful experiment. It necessitated the reduction of the Georgian flower garden to the small area now occupied by the Secret Garden, and in March 1870 the architect, Matthew Digby Wyatt, was involved in a detailed discussion with the landscape engineer, Markham Nesfield, over the execution of a plan for a great new flower garden on the east front. The extensive lawn which hitherto had swept up under the trees of the woodland area was now to be excavated and curtailed by a buttressed brick wall with flights of steps and bays for seats. This very considerable undertaking was completed by 1872, but in the interests of economy it had been decided that all the stone ornaments should be added later.

Neither Wyatt nor Nesfield were involved in the layout of the Parterre; this most elaborate pattern of beds, ribbon borders and hedges was entirely Lady Lothian's creation and was carried out by the head gardener, Mr Lyon. The fountain from Oxnead was placed in the centre in 1873. The correspondent of *The*

Garden recalled in 1903 that the late Lady Lothian 'had such a tender heart for the gardeners who had grown old in her service that, instead of pensioning them off, she kept them about the place to do light work'. In this way a staff of 15 gardeners was retained at Blickling until her death.

When the 11th Marquis moved to Blickling in 1932 he inherited a garden whose environment had been adjusted over the centuries to form a kind of micro-climate. The house and its barns provided shelter on the south and west. The 1st Earl's replanted woodland area shielded it from the sharp north and east winds, while the excavated Parterre lay out of reach of the weather's worst onslaughts. These conditions were allied to a deep, well-drained, coarse, acidic, loamy soil (pH 4.5) which compensated for the sparse annual rainfall of 23in, one of the lowest in England.

Two years earlier Christopher Hussey had written critically of Lady Lothian's Parterre in *Country Life*. 'To the modern eye the pattern area is too small in scale. The lines of the design are lost in a multiplicity of dotted beds, beautifully filled but without perceptible relation to each other or to the house.'[7] It was a natural reaction of the period and perhaps something of a consolation to Philip Kerr, who would not have wished to keep the large garden staff necessary for its maintenance. He also had the good fortune at this juncture to meet Norah Lindsay, who is only now achieving recognition as one of the great gardeners of the 20th century. It is conceivable that Kerr met her through the Astors at Cliveden, but her first visit to Blickling was an expedition from Houghton, where she was staying with the Cholmondeleys, in the company of the Kenneth Clarks.

Norah Lindsay's achievements are surprisingly ill-documented but it is evident that much of her life was spent moving from one country house to another making deft and brilliant adjustments to their ancient gardens. At Blickling she always stayed in the Chinese Bedroom and the staff still remember the primrose scent that used to pervade that part of the house after her visits. Her reputation at this stage rested principally on Hidcote in Gloucestershire, where for several years she had been planting with Lawrence Johnston a garden of enduring beauty and fame, and upon her own garden at Sutton Courtenay which she had published in *Country Life* in 1931. She is usually characterised as a disciple of

Gertrude Jekyll and it is clear that she developed Miss Jekyll's ideas on the choice and grouping of herbaceous plants. But she was never hidebound by theory and her approach to the remodelling of the Blickling Parterre and the Temple Walk shows how sensitive she was to their inherent qualities and potential. The yew pillars and 'grand-pianos' of the Parterre she kept, but the conifers which marched in an orderly procession to the Temple and which might have appealed to her love of the Italian tradition she removed, thus immeasurably improving the sense of scale. The Temple was now to be surrounded by azaleas in subtly graded colours, merging into the shade of the overhanging trees. In the Parterre the myriad of minuscule beds was replaced by four large squares banked up into the centre to provide a magnificent display of herbaceous plants in graduated colours, predominantly pink, blue, mauve and white near the house, but yellow and orange to the east. In the shelter of the Parterre's southern wall she made another long herbaceous border whose quieter colours provide a foil for the main beds.

The spring is always rather late in Norfolk and the succession of flowering at Blickling begins in late February with carpets of snowdrops beneath the cherries above the south border. In April the west garden takes over with a great display of daffodils under magnolias. The terrace is also covered with daffodils at this time and in May Mrs Lindsay's azaleas and the Victorian rhododendrons begin to add their colours to the woodland walks. The herbaceous beds flower from June to September and as they begin to fade a border of penstemons (an introduction by the Trust), above the southern terrace, provides a focus of intense colour well into September. Several splendid *Magnolia grandiflora* on the front of the house keep their large pale flowers into the autumn when the softly decaying colours of the native trees and the glowing tones of the red oaks in the arboretum signal the onset of winter and the period when the garden staff, now seven permanent gardeners, undertake some of the major tasks of the year.

The trimming of Blickling's famous yews begins in August with the topiary of the Parterre. The great hedges are not tackled until September when the task is accomplished with mechanical cutters in 'little over a fortnight, but not without scaffolding and constant attention to form and line. Many of the herbaceous cultivars are now rare and in some cases unobtainable, so

(*Right*) The herbaceous beds of the Parterre

In the east lawn at Blickling four square beds are arranged in blocks of carefully graded colour. All are surrounded by a symmetrical planting of roses edged with catmint, with clipped yews marking the corners. Detailed planting plans are shown for the two colour schemes.

KEY North-west Bed

1 *Aconitum × bicolor*
2 *A.* 'Bressingham Spire'
3 *A. napellus carneum*
4 *A.* 'Spark's Variety'
5 *A. vulparia*
6 *Anaphalis margaritacea*
7 *Astrantia major*
8 *A. maxima*
9 *Campanula lactiflora*
10 *C. persicifolia* 'Telham Beauty'
11 *C. trachelium* 'Albo Plena'
12 *Delphinium*
13 *Dictamnus albus purpureus*
14 *Echinops ritro*
15 *Erigeron* 'Quakeress'
16 *Eupatorium purpureum*
17 *Galega officinalis*
18 *Geranium endressii*
19 *Cicerbita plumieri*
20 *Lavatera cultivar*
21 *Leucanthemum maximum* 'Phyllis Smith'
22 *Liatris spicata*
23 *Limonium latifolium*
24 *Lychnis chalcedonica*
25 *Lythrum salicaria* 'Brightness'
26 *L.s.* 'Robert'
27 *Macleaya cordata*
28 *Monarda didyma* 'Cambridge Scarlet'
29 *Phalaris arundinacea* 'Picta'
30 *Phlox* 'E. Campbell'
31 *Bistorta amplexicaulis* 'Atrosanguinea'
32 *B.* 'Superba'
33 *Salvia* 'Superba'
34 *Sanguisorba* sp.
35 *Sidalcea* 'Croftway Red'
36 *S.* 'Croftway Red'
37 *S.* (own)
38 *Stachys olympica*
39 *S. macrantha*
40 *Thalictrum delavayi*
41 *Veronica spicata*
42 *V. virginica alba*
43 *V.v. japonica*
44 *Yucca filamentosa*

KEY North-east Bed

1 *Achillea* 'Coronation Gold'
2 *A.* 'Moonshine'
3 *A. ptarmica*
4 *Aconitum napellus*
5 *Anaphalis margaritacea*
6 *Anthemis* 'E.C. Buxton'
7 *A.* 'Grallach Gold'
8 *Crocosmia paniculata*
9 *Artemisia lactiflora*
10 *Campanula trachelium* 'Albo Plena'
11 *Centaurea macrocephala*
12 *Erigeron* 'Quakeress'
13 *Helenium pumilum*
14 *H.* 'Riverton Gem'
15 *H.* 'The Bishop'
16 *Heliopsis scabra* 'Bladhams'
17 *H.s.* 'Incomparabilis'
18 *H.s.* 'Zinniiflora'
19 *Ligularia dentata*
20 *Lilium × testaceum*
21 *Lychnis chalcedonica*
22 *Macleaya cordata*
23 *Phalaris arundinacea* 'Picta'
24 *Potentilla nepalensis* 'Master Floris'
25 *Rudbeckia fulgida deamii*
26 *R. nitida* 'Goldquelle'
27 *R. maxima*
28 *Sisyrinchium striatum*
29 *Solidago* 'Goldenmosa'
30 *S.* 'Lemore'
31 *Solidago*
32 *Stachys olympica*
33 *Verbascum chaixii*
34 *Yucca filamentosa*

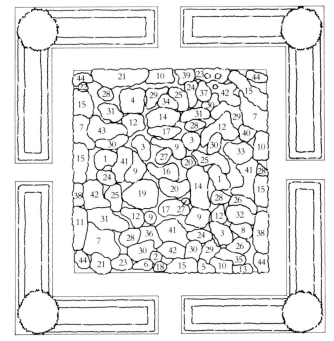

North-west Bed

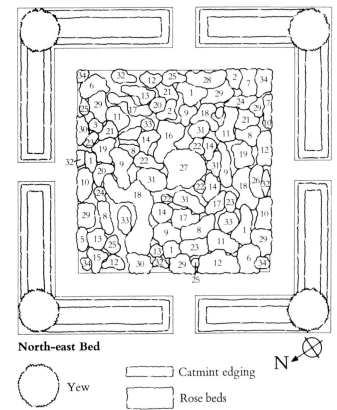

North-east Bed

N

Yew

Catmint edging

Rose beds

the stock is constantly renewed by propagation. Whenever possible the existing planting of the garden is maintained, but observance of historical precedent does not rule out the replacement of plants whose constitution proves incompatible with their surroundings, and in modest ways the creative development of the garden is sustained by new initiatives.

The greatest task which now faces the Trust is the gradual replanting of the formal woodland areas, which are beginning to break up as many of the trees fall prey to disease and old age.

THE YEW HEDGES

In 1745 William Freeman of Hamels described the south front: 'a long Row of Offices and Stables on each side of the Great Court the Lines of which are continued to ye Road by 2 high Yew hedges.'[8] That they have lived so long without losing their shape is partly attributable to the infrequency of heavy snow falls in Norfolk.

CLIMBING PLANTS ON THE WINGS

The walls of the two service wings are clothed with a series of vines, with *Wisteria sinensis* and pears, including the famous Blickling pear that was given an Award of Merit by the Royal Horticultural Society in 1907.

THE MOAT

Although a defensive feature of the medieval house, much of the moat was dry when the Jacobean house was built. Flags were being laid here in 1670[9] and in 1676/77 there is a record of planting out.[10] Water ran in the western arm until the mid 18th century, supplying the 'Wilderness Pond'. The moat walls were rebuilt in 1864 as part of general improvements to the pleasure grounds;[11] the iron railings were supplied in the same year by the estate blacksmith John Salmon.[12] The moat has never proved a particularly hospitable environment for planting. The regime of roses, clematis and bedding out adopted by the Victorians was considerably revised by Norah Lindsay, who introduced much hardier and more abundant plants including hostas, species of hydrangea (*H. H. villosa* and *petiolaris*), as well as buddleias and rosemary.

THE WEST GARDEN

The garden on this side of the house is largely given over to a collection of magnolias. On the west wall of the house are climbing roses with hostas growing at their feet.

THE SHELL FOUNTAIN

This was supplied to Lady Lothian by Austin & Seeley in 1877: '1 Rokeby Shell and 3 legs of Rock £8.10.0.'[13]

THE EAST GARDEN

TERRACES

Plans for the excavation and walling of the Parterre were prepared by Sir Matthew Digby Wyatt in 1870–71. The work was not fully complete until 1877.

GARDEN ORNAMENTS

Thirty pieces were supplied to Lady Lothian by Austin & Seeley of Euston Road in 1877. These included ball finials, vases and sphinxes for the walls and steps.[14] On the Parterre itself, however, only the two tall vases at the eastern end are Victorian; the handsome urns decorated with Vitruvian scroll and the two herms flanking the eastern steps are *c.*1720–30.

THE FOUNTAIN

Set up in its present position in 1873,[15] this 17th-century fountain was one of the objects acquired from the Oxnead sale in 1732. A drawing by Humphry Repton *c.*1780 shows it standing in the Great Wood near Lady's Cottage.

PARTERRE AND BORDERS

Lady Lothian herself designed the first highly complex layout of flower beds whose appearance is recorded in early photographs. It was radically simplified by Norah Lindsay for the 11th Marquis in 1932. She retained the topiary but replaced the intricacies of the Victorian planting with four large herbaceous plots surrounded by beds of old roses and catmint. The planting of the beds is shown diagrammatically opposite.

An Oriental plane

THE ACRE

Until the 1760s this square lawn was the site of the Wilderness Pond (page 56) shown in Prideaux's drawing of *c*.1725. The vast tree with layering branches on the northern edge is a Turkey oak.

THE BASTION

A curving earthwork walled in 1871, this may well be the remnant of the 'mount in the Great Garden' reduced in 1688–89 (page 56), and could therefore be an important survival of the Jacobean garden. The trees are Oriental planes.

THE SUMMER HOUSE

This modest timber structure may well be one of the 2nd Earl's late 18th-century covered garden seats.

THE DOG OF ALCIBIADES

Supplied by Austin & Seeley in 1877 for £7.00.[16]

THE SECRET GARDEN

This occupies part of the site of Lady Buckinghamshire's garden (page 56), a much larger enclosure for which Humphry Repton made recommendations *c*.1800 (page 58). The trellis seat was probably installed for Lady Suffield by John Adey Repton. The garden was reduced to its present shape in the 1860s. The shrub garden by which it is approached from the south was laid out by Norah Lindsay in 1936 and includes *Phormium tenax*, New Zealand flax; *Cornus alba* 'Elegantissima', a variegated, red-stemmed dogwood; *Cornus kousa* (*Benthamidia kousa*); *Hydrangea serrata* (Japan); *Hydrangea arborescens discolor* 'Sterilis' (a native of the USA); *Pseudosasa japonica* (*Arundinaria japonica*) bamboo; *Piptanthus laburnifolius* (*P. nepalensis*) Nepal laburnum; *Choisya ternata* (Mexico), Mexican orange flower; *Magnolia sieboldii* (*M. parviflora*) (Japan, Korea); *Lilium regale* (Sichuan); *Ilex aquifolium* 'Argentea Marginata', a variegated holly.

THE WOODLAND GARDEN

In 1861–64, when the Lothians restored the main elements of the formal plan shown in the Corbridge map of 1729, they treated the walks as avenues of separate species: Turkey oak, lime and beech. Many of the trees were destroyed in the hurricane of October 1987 but the Victorian scheme is being replanted. The central vista to the Temple was planted with the azaleas by Norah Lindsay in 1934. The generous scatter of laurel and rhododendrons throughout the woodland was an important part of the 1860s scheme.

THE TEMPLE

This building is first mentioned in 1738, but the date of its construction is likely to be nearer 1730 (page 29). In the frieze the monograms of Sir John Hobart (later 1st Earl of Buckinghamshire) alternate with the Hobart bull. In 1793 it was furnished with six small painted chairs, one elbow chair, one painted table and a Buzaglo stove.[17]

THE TERRACE

The date of this great earthwork is likely to be slightly earlier than the building of the Temple. Its scale and mass are indicative of its origin in the artillery fortifications of the 16th and 17th centuries. Like its contemporary, the Mount, it provided an elevated view of the extended landscape, in this case across the fields towards the town of Aylsham which, in the 18th century, became an important picturesque element. In 1793 a painted shelter known as the 'Aylsham Bench' stood on the Terrace.[18]

THE TEMPLE AVENUE

An avenue of horse chestnuts, planted by the Lothians, probably in the 1860s.

THE ORANGERY

The site of the Orangery, or 'The Greenhouse' as it was then known, was chosen in 1781 and it was probably built in the following year. The architect is likely to have been Samuel Wyatt (page 40). In 1793 it contained 15 large, 11 young and 6 dwarf orange trees in a variety of boxes and tubs, 3 water pots, a water engine and a brazier.[19] Unheated today, it houses hardier plants.

The statue of Hercules is probably one of Nicholas Stone's figures made for Oxnead in the 1640s (page 56). The majolica plaques in the style of Luca della Robbia are late 19th century.

NOTES

1 Larger was paid £33 16s.

2 The contract drawn up between Sir Henry Hobart and the gardener William Trappit in 1683 (NNRO NRS 11126) mentions the 'Great Garden', 'Ladyes Garden' and, interestingly, 'New Ground Wildernesse'. In 1688–89 when the 'Mount in the Great Garden' was partially flattened a series of brick piers was built in its vicinity (NNRO NRS 16323 32C1). In 1690 Thomas Burrows was paid £24 for a palisade and a pair of great gates (NNRO NRS 16335 32C2).

3 These changes are recorded in the tithe map of 1840.

4 This feature has disappeared.

5 NNRO MC3/100/3, 466 x 4.

6 NNRO NRS 18275, 33B1.

7 *Country Life*, 7 June 1930, p.821.

8 Soane Museum shelf 46A.

9 NNRO NRS 23491, 2103.

10 NNRO NRS 16019 31 F10.

11 NNRO MC3/171.

12 NNRO MC3/167 466 x 7.

13 NNRO MC3/226.

14 Ibid.

15 NNRO MC3/213.

16 NNRO MC3/226.

17 NNRO MC3/338 477 x 8.

18 Ibid.

19 Ibid.

CHAPTER SEVEN

THE PARK AND ESTATE

THE PARK

Although there has been parkland at Blickling since the 12th century when the bishops' park and the knights' park lay on either side of the Great Wood, there is only slight evidence of its appearance, and the earliest coherent visual records of planting date from the early 18th century. The 1729 Corbridge survey portrays a scheme of landscape design that was then in its infancy and the drawings made by Edmund Prideaux in *c*.1725 show stiff little 18th-century figures strutting among trees scarcely taller than themselves.

Whoever designed the early 18th-century park was faced with some considerable challenges, not least of which was its severe reduction in the late 17th century. This, together with the topography, now dictated only one direction in which long avenues could be laid out and that was to the west. So, four great alleys were planted here. Three of them splayed at an acute angle in a 'goose-foot' from a tapering oblong space known as 'the Parade', while a fourth set off on its own in roughly the same direction and collided with the 'goose-foot' outside the park boundary. The extension of avenues into farmland was quite common at this period – witness Charles Bridgeman's huge south avenue at Wimpole Hall in Cambridgeshire – but at Blickling it was indispensable to the impression of scale and distance which the park could not otherwise provide. It is obvious from the map that the goose-foot cut into some mature woodland and that the only other block that remained within the park at this time was in the area now known as Mount Park, where Corbridge shows three ranks of large trees. Even today it is possible to find some ancient chestnuts here. In the valley to the north-west of the Hall the stream which ran from Pond Meadow down to the Bure was dammed to create a 'New Pond', the body of the present lake and, although it is not shown in the survey, the large mount on its northern shore must have been constructed at this time.

These features of the 1st Earl's design form the skeleton of the present park, which is both larger in scale and more informal in design thanks to the work of the 2nd Earl. He continued to purchase adjacent land and in the 1760s began to plant up and cut through his father's formal vistas to create the sort of 'natural' landscape that Capability Brown was making for the Hobarts' Norfolk neighbours at Holkham (1762), Kimberley (1763) and Melton Constable (1764). In these circumstances it would not have been surprising if Brown had worked at Blickling too, but as yet there is no evidence that he did. The recasting of the park was already under way in 1762 when Lord Buckinghamshire wrote to his new wife, Mary Ann Drury, to describe the enlargement of the lake: 'The Bottom of my water is almost cover'd in and the surface increases not quite so fast as the motion of the hour hand of a watch. My Bowling Green looks like an Ant Hill through a microscope, all in motion.'[1]

The lake now became the principal vista of the new landscape, and the view from its northern end was intended as the climax of a journey down the 2nd Earl's new Moorgate carriageway. 'What renders it uncommonly beautiful,' wrote Arthur Young in 1770, 'is the noble accompaniment of wood. . . . Some woods of majestic oak and beech dip in the very water, while others retire gently from it and only shade the distant hills.'[2] The extension of the park to the west provided room for a 'Raceground', watched over by a grandstand in the form of a Gothic tower. On the margin of the Great Wood, which bounded its northern perimeter, rose a thatched *cottage ornée*, whose appearance is recorded in two charming watercolours by Humphry Repton. Repton's possible association with the design of parts of the Blickling landscape also remains a matter for conjecture.

The quiet, undulating parkland of the late 18th century, with its sessile oaks, groves of beech and ancient sweet chestnuts, survives with comparatively few changes.

(*Right*) The lake

POND MEADOW

The impoverishment of the estate in the late 17th century denied the Hobarts the opportunity to make land purchases that would have permitted the diversion of the Aylsham/Saxthorpe road and the joining of Pond Meadow with the rest of the park. This remains, however, the only part of the park to retain the general shape of the 17th-century plantings.

THE ICE HOUSE

Before the invention of the domestic ice box in 1844, ice houses were the only method of keeping perishable provisions at a low temperature. The steward, Robert Copeman, wrote to Lady Buckinghamshire in April 1790, 'There was a great fall of snow this afternoon, as soon as ever it was thick enough I spoke to the Gardeners and had as many Labourers as I could, the Ice House is about half full; the men kept at it to between 9 & 10 o'clock.'[3] It was still in use in the 1930s.

DEER BANKS

These substantial earthworks, a combination of a bank and a sunken fence, were the traditional method for confining deer. Those at Blickling were made by the 1st Earl of Buckinghamshire and mark the boundaries of the early 18th-century park. Two stretches are particularly impressive. One lies between Greenhouse Park and the Aylsham road, the other is found east of the lake near Park Farm.

THE PARADE

Laid out in the early 18th century, the Parade was once an oblong open space tapering to its western end to create an artificial perspective and bounded by walks planted with a mixture of trees. Prideaux's drawing of c.1725 illustrates the north walk and a goose-foot of three avenues which splayed out from its western end. A few individual trees survive but the plan shown clearly in Corbridge's survey of 1729 has been obscured by later plantings.

THE LAKE

Formed before 1729 by the damming of the stream which runs down into the River Bure from Pond Meadow, the lake was extended at its northern end in

Lady's Cottage and the Oxnead fountain, by Humphry Repton, c.1780

the 1740s and towards the house by the 2nd Earl in 1762, only to be pushed back by the 8th Marquis of Lothian in 1863–64. The small circular island was probably made in the 1860s as a roost for water fowl.

THE MOUNT

This early 18th-century feature is part of the 1st Earl's park, as is the Mount Walk, a double line of oaks stretching down towards the Pleasure Grounds and now surviving in fragmentary form. The spiral path of the Mount was once confined by a neat yew hedge which has now grown up to a series of individual trees. The water tank on the summit was built by Maurice B. Adams for Lady Constance Lothian in 1884–85 as part of a fire fighting system for the hall.[4]

THE GREAT WOOD

Since the Middle Ages the Great Wood has occupied roughly its present position. Old deer banks, still traceable in the depths of the wood, indicate its earlier boundaries. There are few really ancient trees. The conifer plantations were introduced after the Second World War and over the last few years the Trust has been gradually replacing them with traditional hardwoods.

LADY'S COTTAGE

Only foundations and some overgrown box mark the site of this little Gothic cottage built for Lady Buckinghamshire in the early 1760s. In 1793 it was furnished with a dining table and chairs as well as an impressive array of cutlery, crockery and cooking equipment.[5]

THE GOTHIC TOWER

This eccentric structure may have been in Lord Buckinghamshire's mind as early as 1758 (page 32). Ceiling joists were being installed in June 1773. Originally whitewashed, it provided an important decorative accent in the park and was used as a grandstand for watching racing. In 1793 it was quite comfortably furnished for this purpose. Carpeted and hung with prints, it contained rush-seated and Windsor chairs as well as a Bath stove and equipment for making tea.[6] It was converted into a house in 1857.[7]

THE MAUSOLEUM

Within a year of the 2nd Earl's death in 1793 his daughter Caroline and her husband William Assheton Harbord (later Lord and Lady Suffield) commissioned Joseph Bonomi to design a mausoleum. In 1796 the present structure, modelled on the Roman pyramidal tomb of Cestius, was begun. The completed Mausoleum was consecrated by the Bishop of Norwich in 1797. Lord Buckinghamshire and his two countesses are buried here.

The Mausoleum

THE ESTATE

The Blickling estate comprises 4,777 acres nestling in a loop of the River Bure including: 500 acres of woodland, 450 acres of parkland, and 3,500 acres of farmland. Soils vary with heavier land towards Aylsham and the river and lighter soils to the west towards Itteringham and Oulton. It is good agricultural land, but not the best in Norfolk, being classified as Grades 2 and 3, compared to Grade 1 for the Fens and the area around the Broads. The estate includes the Buckinghamshire Arms, which was registered as an 'alehouse' and was part of the estate as early as 1616. Since the early 17th century the Hobarts and their successors have also been Lords of the Manor of Aylsham-Lancaster, a procurement which gave the family the market rights and considerable influence in the town.

The estate is clearly no museum piece. It is a social and economic unit, as relevant today as it was in the time of Sir Henry Hobart, the Earls of Buckinghamshire, Lady Suffield and the Lothians. Energetically managed by the National Trust, it provides the income which supports the house, gardens, parks, woods, their specialist staff and all the essential equipment. Management, however, is not easy. The Trust has to reconcile the interests of tenants, the demands of modern agriculture and the need to raise income with the conservation of the landscape and the expectations of the public. To this end the park, ploughed up during the Second World War, has been restored to grassland; shooting is not allowed in the woods and park, and public access has been improved with the creation of new footpaths. At the same time, financial provision has to be made for the erection of new farm buildings and the maintenance of existing ones, many of which are themselves historic buildings of considerable importance. Tenants are encouraged to participate in the preservation of landscape features, and in partnership with the Trust plant trees and hedges. In addition over 100 cottages, many of them fine examples of Norfolk's vernacular architecture, have to be maintained and managed.

The task the estate has to perform today is perhaps more exacting than at any time in its history, for only in the last 50 years have the lands in the Blickling area been expected to support the whole structure. As late as 1932, the Lothians owned 3,500 acres at Hunworth, Stody and Edgefield, near Holt, which had formed an integral part of the Blickling estate since the mid 18th century. Before that, Blickling was the centrepiece of an even larger estate.

When Lord Chief Justice Sir Henry Hobart purchased the Blickling estate from Lady Agnes Clere in 1616, it was a sad remnant of a great estate, which had been owned by some of the most illustrious figures in Norfolk's past. The Cleres in the late 16th century stood second only to the Duke of Norfolk, and possessed estates at Ormesby, Blickling, Thetford and Wymondham, not to mention smaller properties and a residence in London. Their decline in the early 17th century was precipitous, and led to the disintegration of the entire estate by 1623. Sir Henry acquired not only Blickling, but their property at Wymondham, Waborne, Acle, Martham and Somerton, near the Cleres' ancient seat at Ormesby. It was a case of new money acquiring old wealth and all the prestige that went with it. Before this, Sir Henry had also purchased the estates of Sir Thomas Gresham at Intwood, Richard Barney at Langley, Thomas Thetford at Hevingham and Saxthorpe, Sir Charles Cornwallis at Horsham St Faiths, the Earl of Arundel at Methwold and Banham, and Thomas Flowerdew at Hethersett. In addition he had received grants of Crown Land at Cawston and Hevingham Park and, as a special gift, a lease of the prestigious manor of Aylsham-Lancaster (the freehold was secured later). The Corporation of the City of Norwich gave him a 41-year lease of Chapelfield House, which the Hobarts used as their Norwich residence until 1756 when it became the Assembly Rooms. Sir Henry, a formidable operator in the land market, was acutely aware of the prestige value of property. Blickling provided a fitting climax to his career and a worthy seat for his family.

Sir Henry and his son Sir John set about restoring Blickling to its medieval grandeur: a new mansion was built and the park extended and improved. During the 1620s and 1630s Sir John purchased about 200 acres to the east of the hall, on the Aylsham side, much of which was described as having been 'in the park'. This indicates the level of deterioration that had occurred during the final years of Sir Edward Clere, and might have ended with disparkment, but for Sir Henry's timely intervention. In 1633 Sir John obtained a licence from the King 'to empark, to fence and pale 500 acres of his own land and stock it with wild beasts'.

This renaissance did not last long. By the 1660s the Hobarts were in financial difficulties caused by their extravagance and intemperate involvement with politics. Properties were sold and mortgaged, while the estate at Blickling had to be more intensively managed. During the 1670s and 1680s, the heathland to the west of the park was ploughed up and enclosed, while much of the parkland between the Great Wood and the Hall was divided into farms. This period of retrenchment is immortalised on the estate map of 1729 which shows long avenues and formal tree planting superimposed on farmland. Only two farmhouses survive from this period of retrenchment, Park Farm and what is now the Old Rectory. Both were built by the 3rd Baronet, and have the iron letters 'JH' firmly attached to their gables. Another, Moorgate Farm, by the common to the north of the park, was almost completely rebuilt in the 19th century, while two further farms in the park have disappeared.

Prosperity returned to Blickling in the 1720s and 1730s, first with the marriage of Sir John Hobart to Judith Britiffe, heiress to Robert Britiffe of Hunworth, and secondly through the influence of Henrietta Hobart, now Countess of Suffolk, who secured lucrative court appointments and a peerage for her young brother. Britiffe, who was also Sir Robert Walpole's family lawyer, managed his son-in-law's affairs with great sagacity. He purchased much of the outstanding land in Blickling: Hall Farm, Flashpit Farm and Silvergate Farm; farms in Oulton: Green Farm, Wood Farm, Malthouse Farm and Oulton Lodge Farm, and consolidated his own estate at Hunworth and Stody, which he left to his grandson, John Hobart, the 2nd Earl of Buckinghamshire. Remaining portions of old Sir Henry Hobart's estate at Langley, Wymondham and Wood Dalling were either sold or left to the younger children of the 1st Earl by his second marriage. Intwood, however, with its adjoining property at Keswick, remained part of the Blickling estate until 1793 when these two units were sold individually to the Musketts and the Gurneys.

John Hobart, 2nd Earl of Buckinghamshire, consolidated the estate in the second half of the 18th century with acquisitions in Aylsham, including Valley, now called Manor, Farm from the Robins family and Old Hall, which he seems to have purchased from Thomas Wyndham of Cromer in 1751. This process of consolidation in the Blickling area was greatly advanced by the marriage of Lord Buckinghamshire's daughter Caroline – who was also to become his heiress – to her neighbour William Assheton Harbord of Gunton, later Lord Suffield. On Harbord's death in 1822 he left his property in Itteringham, Erpingham and Ingworth to his widow and it became permanently attached to the Blickling estate. In 1839 she purchased the Blickling Lodge Estate at auction in the Castle Hotel, Norwich. Apart from a few later acquisitions by Constance, Lady Lothian, such as Abel Heath Farm, the Blickling estate left by Lady Suffield in 1850 was very much the estate as it is today.

The passing of the estate to the Lothians caused Blickling to become a backwater. This was probably an advantage, as it saved the estate from the depredations of profligate heirs, and the enthusiasms of improving landowners. It is significant that Blickling, unlike its neighbour at Felbrigg, has little that could be termed 'estate architecture', except for a few farmhouses – Oulton Lodge, Middle Farm and Mill Farm – and half a dozen cottages erected by Lady Lothian. For the most part, the farmhouses, cottages and buildings still bear the marks of their yeomen ancestry, with the iron initials of long forgotten builders fixed to the gable ends. This gives the estate immense variety and also provides an unusually complete picture of vernacular Norfolk architecture.

GUIDE TO THE BUILDINGS OF THE ESTATE

Short descriptions of some of the more important buildings and features of the estate are given on the following pages. The great majority of the buildings described are in private occupation and may only be viewed from the roads and public footpaths.

THE HALL FARMYARD

An L-shaped range of agricultural buildings on the east side of the west wing which itself incorporated the remains of a 'ragstone barn' when first built in 1623–24. The two brick barns have been much altered, especially during the last war by the RAF. The older of the two barns runs at right angles to the wing and there are small quantities of pre-Jacobean brickwork in its northern wall. Its western gable matches those of the wings and it has a fine arch braced timber roof. The longer barn which runs across its eastern end is probably the 'Great Barn' that was the subject of extensive repairs in 1709–10,[8] of which the arched openings of the east wall probably formed a part.

THE VILLAGE OF BLICKLING

Since the 17th century the village of Blickling has been concentrated in two areas, one round the church and the other at the park gates. The cottages which run at right angles to the church are shown as one house in the Corbridge survey of 1729. In those days the road passed between the church and the forecourt of the hall. The village was then occupied by agricultural workers, smallholders and weavers of worsted and dornick. The gable of the rectory rebuilt in 1868[9] has J.H. in iron letters, probably the initials of the 3rd Baronet (1627–83) in whose time it was the principal farmhouse of the estate. No. 8 Park Gates is a rare survival of the mud wall and thatch cottages that were once, according to the valuation of 1756 (page 30), extremely numerous. Together with No. 5 it was restored as a *cottage ornée* by J. A. Repton in 1830. Later in the century the cottages near the gates were gradually rebuilt with elaborate barge boards and other features designed to make a picturesque approach to the park. The prettiest of the village buildings is the school, built in 1867–68. An alehouse is recorded at Blickling in the early 17th century, but the Buckinghamshire Arms and its handsome barn were built in their present form around 1700.

No.8, Park Gates, Blickling

THE CHURCH

This building does not belong to the National Trust, but contains much that is directly associated with the Hall and its owners. A guide to the church is available in the building.

The south door, through which one enters, is 13th century and the oldest feature in the building which is largely a 15th-century structure. The church was restored in 1872 and 1876 by G. E. Street for Lady Lothian and he is usually cited as the designer of the tower which was built in 1876. It does, however, have much in common with the work of William Butterfield.

MONUMENTS

At the east end of the south aisle is the fine brass of *Sir Nicholas Dagworth* (d. 1401), who built a major house at Blickling, *c*.1390.

There are a number of brasses to 15th-century members of the *Boleyn family* who owned Blickling in the late 15th and 16th centuries.

Next to the Dagworth brass, the monument of *Sir Edward Clere* (d. 1605); a late Elizabethan alabaster chest from which the effigy has been lost and whose flanks are decorated with a fanciful heraldic pedigree tracing the Clere descent back to 1066. Much of the original polychrome remains. It was Clere's widow who sold Blickling to Sir Henry Hobart.

On the south side of the chancel a mural monument with a kneeling effigy of *Elizabeth Gurdon* (d. 1582), erected at the expense of Sir Edward Clere because she caught the cold which caused her death while visiting him. The monument to *James Hobart*, second son of the 3rd Baronet, dates from 1670.

Nineteen members of the Hobart family are buried in the vault beneath the north aisle and on the wall of the south aisle is a monument to *Brigadier John Hobart* and *Thomas*, his brother, both sons of the 5th Baronet, who erected the memorial in 1742.

On the north wall of the chancel is a Gothic monument to the *7th Marquis of Lothian* (d. 1841) by Edward Blore, 1842, and next to the vestry door, a monument to *John Hargrave*, son of the rector, James Hargrave. He was apprenticed in 1627 to a London joiner and Sir John Hobart paid the rector's travel expenses when he took his son up to London to be bound. A decade later Hargrave was working as a carver assistant to the London sculptor, Nicholas Stone. Cutting marble effigies was his speciality and in 1639 he executed the figure of Sir Edward Coke, the great lawyer and statesman, for the monument erected at Tittleshall church, not many miles from Blickling.[10] His premature death in 1640 cut short a promising career and the inscription calls him 'a most curious and excellent workman'.

In the nave the *8th Marquis of Lothian* (d. 1870). His effigy, with life-size angels at the head and feet, was carved by G. F. Watts in 1878. The tomb chest is by J. H. Pollen.

On the south wall of the nave is the memorial to *William Assheton Harbord, Lord Suffield* (d. 1821).

Next to the south door is a white marble relief to *Constance, Marchioness of Lothian* (d. 1901) carved by A. G. Walker; in the background is depicted part of the great garden which she created at Blickling in the 1870s.

The south chapel was fitted out in 1931 as a memorial to *Zelia K. Hoffman*, tenant of Blickling between 1920 and 1929.

STAINED GLASS

East window, a memorial to Lady Suffield, built to William Butterfield's design and glazed by John Hardman in 1856 (page 43). In the centre of the window, *St Andrew with the Evangelists to either side*. Below, scenes from the *Passion*. In the roundel, *The Resurrection*. 'Draw this window boldly,' wrote Butterfield to Hardman in 1854. 'Using lines of some strength and avoiding strong shadows. Remember . . . the *principles* of *early* glass which are the only principles of *all time*' (note 3, page 49).[11]

South chancel window, *Christ appearing to the Apostles* by Clayton and Bell; a memorial to the 8th Marquis of Lothian, installed in 1877 'by friends, tenants and cottagers'.

North chancel window, by Clayton and Bell. Installed in 1877 by Constance, Marchioness of Lothian in memory of her mother-in-law Cecil, Marchioness of Lothian.

THE ORGAN

The Snetzler organ of 1762 was removed from the 2nd Earl of Buckinghamshire's Organ Chamber at the Hall in 1858.[12]

THE ROOD SCREEN

Designed by John Adey Repton in about 1830. He produced designs for the completion of the tower at about this time.

HERCULES WOOD

Takes its name from a Herculean temple referred to in 1793 but now completely vanished.[13]

THE BRICKYARD

The large kiln, now partially obscured by undergrowth, was probably built in 1862.[14] The estate brickmaker, James Applegate, produced 163,000 bricks from it in 1864 to meet an exceptional demand caused by the rebuilding of the lake wall and improvements to the pleasure grounds which included the revetting of the moat (page 63). The construction of new buildings at Malthouse Farm, Oulton, used 103,000 bricks in 1860 and the Brickyard stock book of 1860–65 records a useful range of paviour, drainage pipes, copings and other items needed on the estate.

SILVERGATE

A hamlet of estate cottages. Most houses on the estate were probably thatched until the end of the 18th century and one long terrace of thatched cottages survives here. In some of the tiled cottages it is possible to see on the gable ends the line of the steeper pitch from the days when they were thatched. Iron initials on various gables refer to the owners of the properties, such as James Sayer and John Aldridge, prior to their acquisition by the 1st Earl of Buckinghamshire in the mid 18th century. The estate sawmill was located on the west side of the settlement. A new 8 horse-power steam sawmill was purchased by Lord Lothian in 1854.[15]

Aylsham Old Hall *c.*1690, from an overmantel picture in the house

ABEL HEATH

The 1729 survey shows Abel Heath farm as an impressive house with projecting wings. Some of this structure probably remains in the present, more modest house. Abel Heath itself was traditionally a common. Its undulating character was caused by uncontrolled gravel extraction in the 19th century which by 1852 had made it hazardous to traffic.[16]

AYLSHAM OLD HALL

The date 1689 in iron letters on one of the chimneys records the completion of this impressive house. It may have been constructed by the master bricklayer who built the west wing of Felbrigg to the designs of William Samwell in 1687: the curved door pediment and moulded string course are identical. The house was probably built by a branch of the Windham family who owned Felbrigg,[17] and was acquired by the Blickling estate in 1751. An important contemporary panel painting, built into the panelling of a first-floor room, records the house at its completion, surrounded by a formal garden in the Dutch style with a canal and an avenue, both of which survive today. In the late 18th century Robert Copeman, the 2nd Earl's agent, lived here. The large barn with its elaborate gable is one of the many Norfolk buildings to register the influence of the wings at Blickling. The hall was given new

Park Farm

windows and a slate roof in the early 19th century. The original fenestration may be seen on the west side. The pantiles were restored by the Trust.

FLASHPIT FARM

The farmhouse now has the appearance of a late 18th-century building but the core of the house may be 17th century. The present main façade has reversed the orientation of the house, which originally faced north-east. The long barn in the centre of the more recent farm buildings is 18th century.

PARK FARM

The core of the tall farmhouse may be one of only two buildings on the estate that can be ascribed to the period of the 3rd Baronet, who died in 1683. His initials appear on one of the gables. It has a particularly well-preserved group of farm buildings, the oldest of which are 18th century.

AYLSHAM MARKET PLACE

The Trust has inherited the Lordship of the Manor of Aylsham-Lancaster and the Market Place remains an outlying portion of the estate. It is surrounded by distinguished 16th-, 17th-, and early 18th-century buildings.

THE BUTTLANDS, AYLSHAM

This strip of land, also part of the Lordship, was used for archery practice in the Middle Ages following the statute of Edward III in 1363 which required archery to be practised on Sundays and holidays. Originally the range would have been 220 yards long to meet the minimum statutory length for longbow practice.

BLICKLING LODGE

This large red brick house on the northern outskirts of Aylsham was built by George Hunt Holley, an Aylsham solicitor, in 1787 and purchased by Lady Suffield in 1839.[18]

MANOR FARM, AYLSHAM

An ancient farmhouse whose diapered southern gable and lofty chimneys are early 17th century. The east elevation was completely refronted in the early 19th century.

OULTON LODGE

A distinctive Victorian house with decorative barge boards and tall star-topped chimneys like that of Blickling village school, it dates from the early 1860s.

WOOD FARM, OULTON STREET

An early 18th-century farmhouse which retains its original fenestration.

MALTHOUSE FARM, OULTON STREET

The thatched farmhouse is probably one of the oldest domestic buildings on the estate and may be late 16th century. The extensive range of Victorian cattle sheds was built by Lord Lothian in 1860 (page 71).

HILL FARM, ITTERINGHAM

A good early 18th-century farmhouse with shaped gables dated and initialled 'I F 1704'. In the farmyard is an interesting combined granary and cart lodge, the lone survivor of a type of building once common on the estate. The 1756 valuation lists several of them (page 30).[19]

Manor Farm, Itteringham

MANOR FARM, ITTERINGHAM

This distinctive farmhouse has the initials of its builder, Thomas Robins, and the date of its construction, 1707, carved into the keystones of its window heads. The mullioned and transomed windows are original, and the heavy curved door pediment, like that of Aylsham Old Hall, suggests the influence of the west wing at Felbrigg (page 74). The hill behind the house is planted as a small piece of parkland and surmounted by an octagonal gazebo which Robins built in 1765. His land was bought by the Blickling estate c.1800.

NOTES

1 NNRO MC3/284 467 x.

2 Arthur Young, *A Tour of the Eastern Counties*, 1770.

3 NNRO MC3/365 467 x.

4 NNRO MC3/547 & RIBA *Journal*, 3rd series Vol. 1, No. 6 1894.

5 NNRO MC3/338, 477 x 8.

6 Ibid.

7 NNRO MC3/135.

8 NNRO MC3/55 466 x 2.

9 NNRO NRS 18276 33B1.

10 *Walpole Society*, Vol. VII.

11 Paul Thompson, *William Butterfield*, 1971, p. 464. (See also p. 43.)

12 NNRO MC3/141.

13 NNRO MC3/338 467 x.

14 NNRO MC3/156 466 x 7.

15 NNRO MS 18273 33B1.

16 NNRO NRS 18278 33B1.

17 NNRO NRS 1083 25D3.

18 T. Sapwell, *A History of Aylsham*, 1960, p.99.

19 NNRO MC3/252.

CHAPTER EIGHT

TOUR OF THE HOUSE

Exterior

The Jacobean house is built on the site of a late medieval predecessor which determined the proportions and general arrangement of its plan (pages 8–9). Between 1619 and 1626 Sir Henry Hobart rebuilt the south and east fronts. The projecting wings, begun in 1624, also incorporated parts of earlier structures. It was not until the late 18th-century remodelling by the 2nd Earl of Buckinghamshire that all visible trace of the earlier house was removed with the rebuilding of the north and west fronts.

THE SOUTH FRONT

Completed, according to the date stone on the parapet, in 1620. The bulls standing on the bridge are the Hobart crest and more heraldry decorates the arch where two more bulls flank the achievements of Sir Henry Hobart and his wife, Dorothy Bell. The frieze of ox skulls is derived from Palladio but may also refer to the Hobart crest, and it is possible that the spread eagles above the central window refer to the Bell family as well as the Boleyns. The initials H D (for Sir Henry and Dorothy Hobart) and I P for their successors, John and Philippa, decorate lead rainwater goods. On the second floor balcony Sir Henry's legal status is reflected in the statues of Justice, with a sword and scales, and Prudence, with a mirror. On the central gable is a boy with a spear and shield flanked, on the side gables, by Atlas figures which are identical in pose and style to the wooden statues on Robert Lyminge's staircase at Hatfield. The clock tower, built by John Adey Repton after 1828, replaced the 18th-century structure shown in Buckler's watercolour of 1820 (page 82). The Jacobean clock tower is clearly recorded in a drawing of *c*.1750. The clock is by Page and Christian of Norwich, *c*.1780. Repton was also responsible for the colonnades which link the front to its wings. The right-hand colonnade was severely damaged by the collapse of the east wing's north gable in 1853 – signs of rebuilding are detectable.

THE EAST FRONT

The east front is Jacobean throughout its length. On the first floor the windows of the Great Chamber and Long Gallery overlooked the garden and at the ground level were two impressive entrances. One survives beneath the southern colonnade but the position of the other, which opened into the old stairhall, is marked by a solitary rosette in the frieze above the ground-floor windows (page 18). The doorway was removed to the north turret in the early 18th century. The statues on the gables are similar to those of the south front and the plinth of the central one is inscribed 'DONA DEI' ('gift of God'). It may represent Charity. The house's silhouette was enhanced in the 19th century by the raising of many of its chimneys.

THE NORTH FRONT

Prideaux's drawing of *c*.1725 shows how much was left unresolved by the Jacobean design. The square central projection with the shaped gable was probably late 17th century but the straight gables represent Tudor work (page 28), probably built by Sir Thomas Boleyn, that survived until the 2nd Earl's rebuilding of 1767–80. The 18th-century work is unusually faithful to the Jacobean design and only the proportions of the window lights and the glazing bars are indicative of their time. It is not easy to see that only the left-hand gable and turret are actually Jacobean work. The right-hand turret is partly a Tudor survival and is smaller in girth than the other three. Its windows were inserted by the 2nd Earl in 1773. The main room of the ground floor, occupying two of the four 18th-century bays, was Lord Buckinghamshire's organ chamber while the Peter the Great Room and the State Bedroom take up the first floor.

THE WEST FRONT

The Tudor front was remodelled and refaced to a design by William Ivory dated 1765 which was remarkable for its severity and uniformity. The bequest of Lady Buckinghamshire's jewels towards the cost of the project in 1769 is recorded in the central inscription. It was more or less complete in 1771. William Burn, who discovered grave structural defects in 1864, rebuilt the front incorporating gables and other ornaments suggested in a drawing by John Adey Repton dated 1821.

THE WEST WING

The stone bearing the date 1624 is set in a rebuilt gable. Only the much repaired front wall survives from this period. The brickwork is laid in the header bond as distinct from either the Jacobean house (English bond) or the east wing (Flemish bond). The blue brick diapering at the northern end suggests either a change of plan or the existence of an earlier building. The whole of the back was rebuilt by William Burn in 1864 (page 46) to provide improved kitchens, sculleries, a brewery and a laundry. Before the rebuilding it contained a brewhouse, a storehouse for stone, a woodhouse, a glazier's shop, a mortar house and, occupying nearly fifty feet of the southern end, a 'Green House'. It is now occupied by the offices of the National Trust's East Anglian region.

THE EAST WING

The building of this wing is dated by an estimate of 1623 which amounted to £967 10s. It specified a structure 225 feet long and 20 feet wide which included a residential part to the north 120 feet long, all new built, and a stable for 18 horses in the remaining 105 feet, part of which incorporated an old barn. The varied functions were cleverly masked by the brick exterior with its coved plastered 'French eaves' and the four lofty shaped and pedimented gables, or 'Dutch dormers' as the estimate calls them. The stable fittings have not survived but they were to have Doric pillars, the capitals carrying a series of moulded arches, and 'french Racks and maingers with pillars and arches with heele peeses for the horse and bars between them' which the carpenter was to make 'well and workmanlike', 'not much differing from your honnours stable at Highgate'.

The wing retains some of its original internal features, despite a serious fire in 1874. The brickwork may be the earliest dated example of Flemish bond in England. By the late 18th century an apartment at the northern end had become 'the Justice Room', where Blickling's owners would have discharged their hereditary duties as Justices of the Peace. The iron ties in the northern gable forming the initial letters of Henry and Elizabeth Hobart, record its repair in 1695 (page 27). It was rebuilt in 1853. The ground floor of the wing is now used for a restaurant, an information room and a shop and the first floor houses a textile conservation workroom. The 17th-century oak staircase in the central hall came from Drury House, Great Yarmouth, and was installed in 1970. The female statue in the information room is believed to be of Diana and to have come from Oxnead (page 79).

THE ENTRANCE PASSAGE AND THE STONE COURT

The great timber door is much restored but incorporates ancient work. The Entrance Passage ceiling has Jacobean plasterwork. The Stone Court was so called in the late 17th century to distinguish it from the rear courtyard, which was then grassed. The inner arch with its carved stone spandrels, and the date '1619' boldly set in a strapwork panel beneath the Withdrawing Chamber window were both afterthoughts. So was the decoration and enlargement of the front door of the house, now occupying the centre of the north wall but originally specified as 'the porch dore' and set into the left hand of the two turrets. These originally projected into the space of the court but were engulfed by the enlargement of the hall by Lord Buckinghamshire in 1767, when its front wall was realigned further forward. The door was placed centrally in 1695 when the subsidence of the left-hand turret, still noticeable, necessitated repair (page 27).

Initials carved in stone or cut in lead identify the work of different periods. H D and I P are found in the Jacobean sections, but neo-Jacobean B's for Buckinghamshire are found in the frieze and lead down pipes of the rebuilt north wall with its 18th-century Hobart bull. C L on the corner drainpipes stands for Constance Lothian.

Interior

All the contents described are original to the house except where otherwise stated and whenever possible are described CLOCKWISE FROM THE ENTRANCE DOOR under their separate headings.

THE GREAT HALL

The principal room of the Jacobean house, built on the site of the medieval great hall, whose east gable is still concealed behind the right-hand wall. (The screens passage lay to the left and the dais to the right.) It became the stair hall in 1767 when the 1620s staircase was dismantled and reassembled here. The reliefs of Elizabeth I and Anne Boleyn were inspired by the Nine Worthies in the Jacobean hall.

CEILING

A deliberately archaic design of 1767 with the Hobart bull in the centrepiece.

STAIRCASE

Nearly all the Jacobean timbers were embodied in the 18th-century reconstruction. As this was to be painted, the new elements were executed in pine. The newel figures on the left-hand flight, clockwise from the top, are: tall figure with staff, 1620s; soldier with musket and powder flasks, repair c.1650; gentleman in hose, possibly 1620s; at stair foot, bearded soldier in slashed breeches with two-handed sword, 1620s. The other figures, found on the right-hand flight and gallery, are of 1767. They include a soldier in a tricorn, a kilted highlander and a cossack. The decoration of the left-hand newel at the stair foot dates from the 1620s and includes images of night and musical instruments of the period. Its opposite number is decorated with 18th-century instruments.

DECORATION

The present scheme of 1979–80 reproduces the Victorian decoration. In the early 19th century the staircase and reliefs were white and the walls pink.

SMALLER PICTURES

ABOVE THE LEFT-HAND DOOR

Oliver Cromwell, English, 17th century, after Samuel Cooper's miniature in the Buccleuch Collection.

ON THE LEFT PIER

James I, English, 17th century. A small copy of the large state portrait by Daniel Mytens, known only from this and other replicas. From Newbattle Abbey.
The Great Hall, J. C. Buckler, 1820, watercolour.

BENEATH THE LEFT LANDING

1st Duke of Buckingham, English, 17th century. A copy derived from the Mytens full-length of 1626 at Euston Hall, Suffolk.

AROUND THE CENTRAL WINDOW

Sir James Hobart (1436–1507). Attorney-General to Henry VII and Lord Chief Justice Hobart's most distinguished ancestor. An imaginary portrait in the dress of a later period. There is a version in the Norwich Civic Portrait Collection.
Sir James Hobart (1436–1507) *and his wife*. A 17th- or 18th-century copy of a window at Loddon church which commemorates its rebuilding by Sir James. It is shown in the background together with St Olave's Bridge, which was built by his wife.
Sir Henry Hobart, 4th Baronet (1658–98), attributed to William Wissing (1653–87). The victim of the notorious Cawston duel (page 28) and father of the 1st Earl of Buckinghamshire.

BELOW THE LANDING

Henry VIII, after Holbein, English, 16th century, one of several copies of the lost original. From Newbattle Abbey.

ON RIGHT PIER

John, 2nd Earl of Buckinghamshire (1723–93), after Francis Cotes.

ABOVE THE RIGHT-HAND DOOR

General George Monck, English, 17th century, after Samuel Cooper's miniature in the Buccleuch Collection.

FULL-LENGTHS

Twelve of a series mostly commissioned from William Aikman (1682–1731) by Lord Hobart, later 1st Earl of Buckinghamshire, in 1729–32 (page 29). The identity of the sitters derives partly from the 1793 inventory and is tentative.

UNDER LEFT STAIRS

? *Sir Thomas Sebright, 4th Baronet* (1692–1736) or *Mr Crawley*, William Aikman. Sebright was a Tory but his reputation as a book collector perhaps brought him into Hobart's Whig circle. Mr Crawley was mentioned by a visitor who saw these pictures in 1741.

UNDER RIGHT STAIRS

Edmund Prideaux (1693–1745), William Aikman. Identified by the arms on the plinth and the view of Prideaux Place, Padstow. A university friend of Hobart and bibliophile, he drew views of Blickling c.1727 (page 28).

UPPER LEVEL CLOCKWISE

(for portraits on the Staircase Gallery, see page 87)
? *(Sir) John Cope* (1690–1760), William Aikman. Lieutenant-Colonel of the 1st Horse Grenadier Guards at this period. MP for Liskeard in 1727–34 and a political crony of Hobart. He was decisively defeated by the Jacobites at Prestonpans in 1745.
Sir Robert Walpole (1676–1745), William Aikman. The Prime Minister and builder of Houghton Hall; wearing the Chancellor of the Exchequer's robes.
Thomas, Lord Lovel (1697–1776), William Aikman. The builder of Holkham, who became Earl of Leicester in 1744.
Sir William Leman, 2nd Baronet (d.1741 or 44), William Aikman, 1729. Leman held considerable property in Suffolk. He stands before the Piazza at Covent Garden.
General Sir Robert Rich, 4th Baronet (1665–1768), William Aikman, 1729. Of Roos Hall, Suffolk, Rich is shown as a Colonel of the 8th Dragoon Guards. He sat for Hobart's pocket borough in Devon, Bere Alston, in 1724–7 and from 1727 to 1741 he succeeded him as MP for St Ives.
Colonel Harbord Cropley Harbord (?1675–1742), William Aikman. MP for Norfolk 1728–34.
Charles, 2nd Viscount Townshend (1674–1738), studio of Charles Jervas. The noted agricultural pioneer and politician.
William Morden (?1696–1770), William Aikman, 1729. Assumed the name and arms of his uncle Harbord Harbord in 1742, the year in which he began Gunton Hall, where there is a later portrait in a similar frame.

FURNITURE

A series of 17th-century oak elbow chairs of different designs.

Large mahogany side-table in the style of Kent, c.1730.
Oriental lacquered chest on English giltwood stand, early 18th century.
Console table with an eagle support, 19th century.
Richly carved 17th-century Flemish oak cupboard.
Mid 17th-century oak court cupboard with an illusionistic frieze of modillions inlaid in boxwood.
Late 18th-century sedan chair; in which Mary Anne, first wife of the 2nd Earl of Buckinghamshire, is said to have died while crossing Green Park in 1769.
Large mahogany side-table, style of William Kent, en suite with its opposite number but with additional legs to support a marble slab, c.1730.
Wheel-chair that belonged to 8th Marquis of Lothian.

CLOCKS

Bracket clock, c.1740, by Jeremiah Taylor of London, converted in the 19th century to 8-bell quarter-striking.
Mahogany long-case clock with an 8-day striking movement by Benjamin Lockwood of Swaffham, late 18th century.

PORCELAIN

Pair of 18th-century Quianlong Chinese fish bowls on contemporary English giltwood stands.

METALWORK

Two mid 18th-century wrought-iron locksmith's signs, Austrian or south German.

LOBBY

The end of a truncated passage built in 1857–58.

PICTURES

LEFT WALL
Newbattle Abbey, gouache. ?Alexander Nasmyth.
Lady's Cottage, Humphry Repton (page 68).
Highland Scenery, gouache. ?Alexander Nasmyth.

RIGHT WALL
Survey of the Blickling Estate, James Corbridge, 1729.

FURNITURE

Small settle of 1685.

CERAMICS

Large blue and white Chinese vase, 18th century.

THE BROWN DRAWING ROOM

Originally the chapel of the Jacobean house, consecrated 1629. The richly ornamented mouldings of the window bays and skirting may be connected with Matthew Brettingham's work for the 1st Earl, 1745–55. In the 1760s it was given over to Lady Buckinghamshire's dressing room and bed chamber. Opened up into a morning room in 1857, renamed in 1930s.

FIREPLACE

The carved spandrels with angels, c.1400, are thought to have come from Sir John Fastolfe's Caister Castle via the Oxnead sale of 1732. The trophied side pieces and the inner surround date from the early 1770s when the ensemble formed part of the organ room on the north front. It was moved here in 1858. The Fastolfe motto crowns the composition with the Buckinghamshire arms beneath.
Iron fireback, decorated with Moses and the brazen serpent, late 17th century.
Grate, Victorian. Steel and brass fire-irons, 18th century.
Gentleman's fireside companion, south German or Swiss, late 17th century.

DECORATION

Redecorated in 1969 keeping the theme of Lord Lothian's colour scheme of the 1930s, but using Japanese silk wallpaper. The ceiling, inserted in the 1930s, conceals an elaborate painted beam ceiling by J. H. Pollen (page 44). Lord Lothian's curtains (machine embroidery on canvas imitating hand-worked satin stitch) and his carpet remain.

PICTURES

NORTH WALL LEFT TO RIGHT
The impressive collection of Stuart portraits in this room was brought to Blickling by the 8th Marquess of Lothian and his wife Constance Talbot in the late 1850s from Newbattle Abbey, their principal Scottish seat. They make a piquant contrast with the Whiggish portraits which dominate the Buckinghamshires' collection.

ON THE NORTH WALL
Mary Howard, mid-17th century, studio of Van Dyck.
Charles I and Prince Charles, 1633, after Van Dyck. A contemporary copy of Van Dyck's 'Great Piece' of 1632 without the figures of the Queen and Princess Mary.
Queen Henrietta Maria, after Van Dyck.

ON THE SOUTH WALL
An Unknown Girl c.1630, J. M. Wright.
James Stanley [future 7th Earl of Derby] *and his bride, Charlotte de la Tremolle*, painted at The Hague in 1626, attributed to Michiel Miereveldt and Studio.

Constance, Lady Lothian (1836–1901), John Leslie. The picture was exhibited at the Royal Academy in 1866. Lady Lothian was responsible for creating the parterre and terraces in the east garden, visible from this room.
Petrarch, Italian, 16th century.
Louis XI, French, 16th century. Both acquired by the 3rd Earl of Lothian in 1649.

FIREPLACE WALL
Lady Tufton, mid-17th century, manner of Van Dyck.
The Artist with Still Life, Goddard Dunning. Inscribed 'Aetatis 64 1678'.

FURNITURE

Giltwood console table, *c*.1725, in the style of William Kent with a later fossil marble top.
Small pier-glass in a shaped frame, English, early 18th century.
Partners desk, late 18th century.
Lacquered cupboard, late 19th century.
Mirror above, English mid 19th century.
Large gilt console table with veined marble top supplied by William Freeman of Norwich, early 19th century.
Two gilt sconces with light-diffusing reeded glass. Probably 19th century.
Set of mid 18th-century armchairs with cabriole legs and two matching stools with original upholstery in Genoa velvet with woollen fringes.
Two lounging chairs with cane sides, part of a set of dining furniture acquired in the early 19th century.

THE LOWER ANTE ROOM

Originally the lower part of the Jacobean stairwell, this room became the drinking room in 1767 and was hung with full-length portraits. In the 19th century it was a small library and in the 1930s a sitting room. It was redecorated in the 1960s.

TAPESTRIES

Three Brussels tapestries *c*.1700 with rustic scenes after David Teniers; they were probably woven in the workshops of Jodocus de Vos. Reputed to have been given to Sir Robert Walpole by Cardinal Fleury, they were purchased in 1859 from a sale at Wolterton Hall.

PICTURES

ON THE SOUTH WALL
Summer flowers in a terracotta vase, Anton Weiss (1801–51).
Tulips, honeysuckle, paeonies and roses in an urn, Jan Frans van Dael (1764–1840).

ON THE NORTH WALL
Two 19th-century colour prints of *Mary Tudor* and *Mary Queen of Scots* by Henry Shaw FSA, 1882, from Strawberry Hill. *Mary Tudor* after an original by Hans Eworth, then in the possession of the Society of Antiquaries, and *Mary Queen of Scots* after a painting once in the possession of the late Patrick Fraser Tytler.

FURNITURE

Two rococo looking-glasses, mid 18th century.
Satinwood and harewood writing table with tambour front, *c*.1790.
Armchair with elaborately carved back in the style of Giles Grendey, mid 18th century. Cover designed by Anna Wellbourn and made by Austin Snowdon, 1980.
Large lacquered chest, oriental, mid 18th century.
Two small semicircular commodes, continental, late 18th century.
Six high back chairs in the style of Daniel Marot. Bought by Lord Lothian in 1939 from the collection of the Countess of Caernarvon.

THE DINING ROOM

The parlour of the Jacobean house, a room used by the family for informal dining and gaming. In 1765 it was altered and refurnished by the 2nd Earl who was concerned to retain and enhance its ancient character.

CEILING AND FRIEZE

The ceiling was to have been painted with the lives of Cupid and Psyche, which may explain why it is divided into plain fields by the 18th-century moulded plaster beams.

PANELLING

The panelling and doorcases in oak and chestnut are a remarkably effective 18th-century pastiche of Jacobean work. In 1765 Lord Buckinghamshire wrote to Lady Suffolk 'The joiner had put an Earl's coronet over the door; but it is ordered to be changed into a bull. Lady B, and my sister's decency proposed a cow; but to compromise the matter directions are given to make it as much like an ox as heraldry will admit'.

DECORATION

The room was painted in the 18th century and was probably white. The present dark stain is mid 19th century.

THE FIREPLACE

The large oak overmantel dated 1627 bears the arms of Sir Henry Hobart, and his wife Dorothy Bell. The marble fire surround is the 2nd Earl's; its tapered, half pilasters match the timber ones to either side. The white marble was no doubt chosen to match a contemporary off-white colour scheme for the woodwork. Lord Buckinghamshire was at pains to preserve the ancient chimney-piece; it was restored in his time (eg the upper frieze) and possibly again in the 1830s. The register stove of the 1760s has an iron surround and steel grate with fender, fire-irons and trivet of the same date.

PICTURES

Philip Kerr 11th Marquess of Lothian (1882–1940), James Gunn, a posthumous portrait of the donor of Blickling.
Unknown Naval Commander, English, early 17th century.
Sir Philip Sidney, English, early 17th century, after portrait type established by John de Critz, *c*.1585.
Supposed portrait of *Anne of Denmark*, ? John de Critz, early 17th century.
Queen Elizabeth, English, 16th-century. Derived from the Ditchley portrait of *c*.1591.

FURNITURE

D-shaped side-table, late 18th century.
Rosewood circular pedestal table, *c*.1830.
Ten-fold screen in painted and gilt leather with floral decoration on the reverse, oriental, 18th century.
Two side-tables with fret decoration, *c*.1765.
Three brass-bound mahogany wine coolers, *c*.1760.
Small firescreen of the type known as a 'slip screen', early 19th century.
The dining table, *c*.1765, is the 2nd Earl's; some of his chairs are ranged round the table in the window bay. He wrote to his wife in July 1766 'It concerns me to think that as we should want at least thirty chairs for the New Eating Room, it will be impossible to have them made in time this summer. You may however consult Macksted; the seats must be either black hair or black leather'.
The high-backed William and Mary dining chairs are from two different sets acquired by Lord Lothian in 1939.

CLOCK

Long-case clock in a burr walnut case with floral marquetry, by Nathanial Hodges of London, *c*.1690.

TEXTILES

Axminster carpet of Persian pattern, late 19th century.

CERAMICS

Three Quian Long chargers, Chinese, late 18th century.
Set of cut and engraved bowls and glasses, Bohemian, 19th century.
Dinner service, Crown Derby, 19th century.

THE SERVING ROOM

The bolection panelling and fireplace date from the late 17th century when this room was made into a small parlour. By 1793 it had become 'The Confectioner's Room' and was hung with full-length portraits. It became the Serving Room in William Burn's alterations of 1864–65, when the staircase and tunnel were introduced and the sink, dresser and hot cabinet installed.

DECORATION

The present scheme, carried out in 1987, reproduces the Victorian decoration.
The tunnel leads under the entrance passage and directly into the area formerly occupied by the Victorian servants' hall. In those days a subterranean corridor to the left ran from here to the main kitchen in the west wing. These rooms were rearranged by Lord Lothian in the 1930s, but in Burn's remodelling, the area between here and the garden entrance was occupied by the servants' hall and butler's pantry. Beyond the garden entrance lay the lamp room and knife room. On the floor above were the steward's room, the butler's bedroom, the housekeeper's room, the housemaids' sitting room and the still room (formerly the 18th-century kitchen).

KITCHEN

Lord Lothian moved the Kitchen into this part of the house in the 1930s.

FURNITURE

The great table, put together in the 18th century, incorporates three pillar supports, two of which originally formed corner legs of a Jacobean table; possibly the one made for the great chamber by Robert Lyminge in 1627 (page 22). The range by Smith & Wellstood of London was given to Blickling in 1988.

THE BROWN STAIRCASE

Built in 1767 when the grand staircase was installed in the Great Hall. In 1865 Burn carried it down to basement level with stone flights to provide a more effective communication with the private entrance from the west garden.

FURNITURE

Carved wooden seat, late 17th century; similar to the benches in the entrance hall at Dunham Massey, Cheshire.

PICTURES

Six engravings after various *Tudor pictures*, George Vertue, mid 18th century.
The Rev. John Graile, Rector of Blickling, 1674–1732.
John Pym, after Edward Bower.
Unknown man, manner of Sir Peter Lely.
Sir Henry Hobart, 4th Baronet, English, late 17th century (on loan).
Four *Antique Sacrifices* and *Mercury delivering a message to Jupiter and Juno*, Francis Hayman. These grisailles, which formed part of the 1st Earl's decoration in the Long Gallery (page 30), are derived from engravings of four reliefs on the Arch of Constantine in Rome and another in the Museo Angelonio, contained in Bellori and Santi Bartoli's *Admiranda Romanarum . . . Monumenta* (*c*.1693).

THE LOTHIAN ROW

This wing, which retains survivals of the old Tudor west range, was fitted out by Lord Buckinghamshire in 1773. The bedrooms on the top floor were each known by a letter of his title, a precedent followed by the Lothians when they refurnished the bedrooms of the second floor. In 1858 Duppa and Collins of London provided wallpapers and matching chintzes. A lily of the valley pattern was used for the curtains, carpets and papers of most of the rooms but 'T', as shown in an early 20th-century photograph, was done out in holly. The furniture, large 'white enamel' pieces lined in birds-eye maple with chintz panels, was supplied by G. E. Burrell of Aylsham in 1861. The bedrooms were redecorated in the 1930s by the 11th Marquis in plain colours; L and O in blue, T in peach, H I A and N in green, and have all since been redecorated and refurnished.

CORRIDOR

PICTURES

Eight drawings by Christoph Heinrich Kniep (1755–1825), Goethe's travelling companion on a visit to southern Italy and Sicily in 1787.

LEFT-HAND SIDE
The Temple at Paestum; The Theatre at Taormina; Mount Etna; A shepherd by a ruined colosseum; Figures and classical ruins by a lake; The temple at Agrigentum.

RIGHT-HAND SIDE
Temple of Vesta at Tivoli; The Bay of Naples.

NEAR THE PRINT ROOM DOOR
Two paintings of *Unknown Men*, English, 17th century.
The South Front of Blickling Hall, J. C. Buckler, 1820.
The East Front of Blickling Hall, J. C. Buckler, 1820.

FAR END
Jedburgh Abbey, Thomas Girtin (1756–1812). The barony of Jedburgh is a Lothian title. The 8th Marquis was buried there in 1870.
Four hand-coloured engravings of *Roman wall paintings*, 18th century.
Neapolitan fan membrane, decorated with Roman subjects.

TAPESTRIES

Two Brussels verdure tapestries, early 18th century.

CLOCK

Eight-day striking long-case clock by John Scott of Edinburgh, *c*.1810.

STAIRCASE GALLERY

(*see page 87*)

'O' ROOM

In 1793 this was Lady Belmore's dressing room, originally the centre of a suite of three rooms (page 38).
The white and Siena marble fireplace, *c*.1773, is by John Ivory, contemporary Carron grate.

DECORATION

The wallpaper, a copy of an early 20th-century French paper, was hung in 1974.

PICTURES

The 8th Marquis of Lothian (1832–70), George Richmond, black and white chalk. A study for the portrait exhibited at the Royal Academy in 1858.
Lisa, 1867, Val Prinsep; a scene from Boccaccio's *Decameron*.
Three watercolours by Louisa Stuart, Marchioness of Waterford (d.1891), Constance Lothian's aunt: *Dancing putti*; a sketch for *The miraculous draught of fishes*; *The Madonna and Child*.
The Crucifixion, Marchigian School, *c*.1500. No doubt bought by the Lothians in Italy in the 1860s.
Blakeney Church 1840 and *Yarmouth Beach*, watercolours, Miles Edmund Cotman (1810–58).

FURNITURE

Victorian iron and brass bedstead with an unusual mid to late 18th-century quilted chintz counterpane (given to Blickling).
The late 18th-century mahogany polescreen contains a

piece of ancient black velvet worked with the legend 'A piece of the bed in which Anne Boleyn was born at Blickling 15... Beheaded 19th May 1536'. The fabric is in fact of the 1560s. A facsimile of this fragment is in the Stranger's Hall Museum, Norwich.
Embroidered prie-dieu, mid Victorian.

CERAMICS

Large wash-stand set by Copeland, 19th century.

PRINT ROOM

A bedroom in the early 1770s, this was known as the 'Copperplate Room' in 1793. The prints found in the 'A' room in 1974 were moved here, probably their original home, and put up with additional borders and decorative devices copied from originals found under layers of paint in the 'A' room. The background is the colour of the original canvas. There are 52 18th-century prints. Several are by Piranesi, including the *Tomb of Cestius* which may have provided a model for the 2nd Earl's mausoleum (page 69). Others are engraved after works by Rubens, Raphael, Claude, Angelica Kauffmann, Reynolds and Richard Wilson.

FIREPLACE

Marble surround by John Ivory, *c*.1773, with a more elaborate Carron grate than its counterpart in the adjacent dressing room.

FURNITURE

Two painted armchairs, late 18th century restored in 1978.
Rosewood pole screen with canvas embroidered panel, late 18th century.
Three neo-Greek chairs painted in black and gilt, early 19th century.
Spinet by Thomas Barron of London, 1724 (on loan).

TEXTILES

Modern festoon window curtain as described in 1793 inventory.
Carpet, Tabriz *c*.1900.

CERAMICS

Two biscuit ware ornaments, late 18th century.
Staffordshire cache pot, 19th century.

LOTHIAN ROW BATHROOM

Redecorated in 1972 with a reprint of an 18th-century paper border. This room originally served as a dressing room to the West Turret Bedroom beyond and probably became a bathroom in 1858–61. The fire surround with a steel shuttered grate is mid 19th century.

PICTURES

The 6th Marquis of Lothian, early 19th-century mezzotint on glass.
Pair of engravings, *Les Chanteuses du Mois de May* and *La Petite Fête Imprevue*, S. Freudenberger, 18th century.
Four prints of *Peasant costume*, C. von Mechel.
La Solfatara, gouache, 18th century.

FURNITURE

Weighing chair by Youngs of London, late 19th century.
Bath, late 19th century.
Mahogany water closet, 1860s.
Oval mirror, late 18th century.
Oval mahogany table with brass mount and marble top, French, 19th century.

WEST TURRET BEDROOM

The principal bedchamber of the Jacobean house, updated *c*.1760. In 1793 it was known as the blue room and traces of the dark blue paint, predating the Georgian woodwork, have been found under the wallpaper. A doorway with stout oak chamfered jambs was uncovered in the north wall, no doubt a Jacobean door communicating with the Tudor west range.

CEILING

A fine Jacobean design of straps and bosses, the cornice may have been remodelled in the 1760s.

FIREPLACE

Carved pine rococo surround of the 1760s. The Carron grate was inserted in the 1770s.

PICTURES

Classical Landscape, attributed to F. Mola, 17th century.
OVER FIREPLACE

Chelsea from the Thames, Antonio Canaletto. The left half of a view painted 1746–48. It shows from left to right, the greenhouse of the Physic Garden; part of Paradise Row;

Turret House (with cupola); Gough House; Sir Robert Walpole's green house, art gallery and casino; and one end of the Chelsea Hospital.

A View of the Rialto, manner of Michele Marieschi, Dutch, 18th century.

Blackfriars Bridge, in the manner of Samuel Scott. Painted in the 1760s when the bridge was nearing completion.

The Bay of Naples, two gouaches, 18th century.

Muskau Castle, Silesia, John Adey Repton, c.1821, who was much employed by Lady Suffield at Blickling in the 1820s and travelled to Prussia to work for Prince Pückler Muskau. This unexecuted scheme was based on German 16th century examples and takes details from Blickling.

FURNITURE

Chippendale mahogany dressing-table with lift-up top and compartments for powder, brushes etc, c.1760.

Walnut stool, late 17th century.

Chest of drawers on stand with floral marquetry, Dutch, late 17th century.

Escritoire inlaid with floral marquetry in various woods, Dutch, late 17th century. Both Dutch pieces much altered in the 19th century.

Wash stand, mahogany, early 19th century.

Lord Castlereagh's brass-bound mahogany dressing-case, early 19th century.

TEXTILES

The modern bed and the window are hung with late 17th- or early 18th-century crewel work discovered in the attics by Lord Lothian. Crewel work is a mixture of many different stitches worked on a union fabric of linen and cotton in crewel wool, a hard-wearing two-ply worsted. Two distinct sets of hangings are discernible. The side curtains are the earlier; dating from the late 17th century they remain in their original state. The backing fabric of the later set was replaced in 1980.

CLOCK

Eight-day spring clock in mahogany case by Alexander Leroux, London c.1820.

WEST TURRET BATHROOM

The closet of the Jacobean bedchamber, it became a bathroom in the 1860s. The plaster ceiling is Jacobean. Pine fire-place 1760s, Carron grate 1770s.

PORCELAIN

Mirror (Meissen, 19th century), shepherdesses (Vincennes) and accessories.

THE CHINESE DRESSING ROOM

The room formed the western part of the Jacobean withdrawing chamber, divided into a bedroom and dressing room by Lord Buckinghamshire in the early 1760s. The pine chimney-piece is of this date, the grate of the 1770s.

DECORATION

The room was originally decorated with a Chinese wallpaper, fragments of which were discovered during redecoration in 1972–73. The present paper is a modern reprint of an English paper of 1760.

PICTURES

Amelia Anne Hobart, Countess of Londonderry (1772–1829), after Sir Thomas Lawrence. The sitter was the youngest daughter of the 2nd Earl and married Viscount Castlereagh, 2nd Marquis of Londonderry, in 1794.

The Children of the 3rd Baronet, four small paintings on panel, late 17th century.

Interior with Figures, Bartholomeus van Bassen (1590–1652).

NORTH WALL

Four framed *Fragments of the 18th-century Chinese wallpaper*.

Elizabeth Fortescue, Countess of Ancram (1745–80), Sir Joshua Reynolds, painted 1769. Lady Ancram's son, the 6th Marquess of Lothian, married Harriet, Lord Buckinghamshire's eldest daughter, in 1793. The picture has a fine rococo frame. Bequeathed to the Trust by Lady Mildred Fitzgerald in 1969.

Figures examining an antique statuette by candlelight, 17th century, in the manner of Gerard van Honthorst. The figure on the left may be a self-portrait. The two figures on the right are derived from one model.

Portrait of the artist's wife and son, Benjamin West, contemporary with a version exhibited in the Royal Academy in 1770.

An Unknown Girl, Dutch, 17th century.

Lady as a Shepherdess, Caspar Schmitz, late 17th century.

EAST WALL

Lady Martha Drury and her daughter Mary, Countess of Buckinghamshire, 1754, attributed to John Astley. Mary married the 2nd Earl of Buckinghamshire in 1761 and died in 1769, bequeathing her jewels for the completion of the west front. The carved frame is contemporary.

SOUTH WALL

An Unknown Woman, J. B. Gaspar, 1690.

Emma, Countess of Brownlow (d.1872), pastel. She was the daughter of the Earl of Mount Edgecumbe and granddaughter of the 2nd Earl of Buckinghamshire.

FURNITURE

17th-century Italian chest on late 18th-century English stand. Drawers fitted with plaques of 'ruin' marble.

Large floral marquetry cabinet, Dutch, c.1680 in the style of Van Mekeren, with evidence of considerable 19th-century alterations.

Inlaid chest on carved stand. The chest possibly north African or Hispanic, the stand English or Dutch; 19th century.

Four high-back chairs in the Dutch style with seats worked in gros point and flame stitch, Victorian.

THE CHINESE BEDROOM

Formed in about 1760 by partitioning the Jacobean withdrawing chamber, the room had a window overlooking the Stone Court which was blocked up in the 1760s but still retains its masonry and glazing on the exterior. While the ceiling is typically rococo, the frieze is neo-Jacobean and imitates the ornaments of the two stone Jacobean doorcases on the staircase landing.

WOODWORK

The chimney-piece, including the basket of flowers in the broken pediment, is of carved pine, c.1760. (The grate is early 1770s.) The doors and dado panelling are of the same period.

DECORATION

When Lady Beauchamp Proctor visited in 1764 she remarked that most of the apartments were hung with 'India paper' and it is clear that the Chinese wallpaper dates from the construction of the room. The two deep patterned borders at top and bottom are European. The piece in the overmantel is noticeably different in colour and design from the hangings of the walls.

FURNISHINGS

Bedside tables: a pair of Sheraton enclosed wash-stands c.1800.

The bed is c.1760. Its hangings are an extremely rare survival of a Norwich shawl bedspread cut up and displayed in the 1930s by the 11th Marquis. Originally these pieces formed a large counterpane of a type for which P. J. Knights was awarded a silver medal from the Society of Arts in 1792. These counterpanes were woven 4 yards wide without a seam. This one had a border of coats of arms (the present valance), and in the central field were the arms of Lord Buckinghamshire and Caroline Conolly (the present headboard) with Hobart bulls in the corners. The four bulls are now in the Blickling textile conservation room, the Strangers' Hall Museum, Norwich, and the Victoria and Albert Museum, London.

Under the modern counterpane is another rare survival, a 'rosed' or 'cornered' blanket. Between c.1700 and c.1820 blankets had corner motifs worked in long stitches of homespun worsted, generally by the weavers' wives. They were paid 'a halfpenny a piece' according to Arthur Young. This blanket is the best of three at Blickling.

Mahogany corner dressing-table in the style of Gillows of Lancaster c.1810.

Carved ivory pagodas, Chinese, 18th century, believed to have come from Marble Hill (page 30).

Unusual white japanned wardrobe with *chinoiserie* designs in green similar in its decoration to the suite made by Thomas Chippendale for David Garrick's house in the Adelphi, early 1770s.

Early 18th-century lacquered chest on giltwood stand.

Oval lacquer sweetmeat box on stand, oriental, early 19th century.

Octagonal gilt mirror, c.1790.

Finely carved chair derived from one of the patterns in Chippendale's *Director* of 1754.

CARPETS

Unusual and important Axminster carpet, late 18th century.

Hearth rug: a Ghiordes Moslem prayer rug.

THE SOUTH DRAWING ROOM

This was the great chamber of Sir Henry Hobart's house. It opened directly off the Jacobean staircase, a common arrangement in great houses of this date. It was converted into a drawing room by the 2nd Earl in about 1760. Charles II was entertained here in 1671 and it was much used by the 11th Marquis who held meetings at the large mahogany table (page 49).

CEILING

One of the best Jacobean ceilings in the house. Edward Stanyon's agreement dated 1620 reveals that 'for frett ceiling . . . in the gallery, greate chamber, withdrawing chamber and parlor at Blickling' he was to be paid 'fyve shillings six pence a yard square measure according to such plotts and workmanship directed to me [by] Robert Lyminge his Lordship's Surveyor of the said work'. The frieze appears to have been altered in the 18th century.

THE CHIMNEY-PIECE

The best surviving Jacobean chimney-piece at Blickling; designed and executed by Robert Lyminge, it was originally painted to resemble different marbles. The stone surround is also Jacobean. The cast iron fireback has the arms of Elizabeth I; the burnished steel grate is late 18th century.

PANELLING

Dado panelling, neo-Jacobean, early 1760s.

DECORATION

The room was transformed by the 11th Marquis in the 1930s. The woodwork, which had been given an oak stain by the Victorians, was stripped and the walls hung with the present painted canvas.

PAINTINGS

Sir Henry Hobart, 1st Baronet (d.1626) English, 17th century, after Mytens. A copy of the important portrait which hangs in the State Bedroom (see p.89).
Henrietta Howard, Countess of Suffolk (c.1688–1743), attributed to Thomas Gibson. One of the most important figures in the history of Blickling (page 30), she is shown in masquerade dress. Painted c.1720 and later incorporated into the 1st Earl's series of full-length portraits.
Sir John Maynard (1602–90), attributed to Henry Tilson. Maynard was Sergeant to Cromwell and Charles II and became Lord Commissioner of the Great Seal in 1689. His grand-daughter, Elizabeth, married the 4th Baronet and was the mother of the 1st Earl. The picture was reframed in the early 1720s with the rest of the set.
An Unknown Man, manner of Sir Peter Lely.
Lady Dorothy Hobart, 1634. Attributed to the Master V. M. Dorothy was the widow of the 1st Baronet.
? Jocosa Drury, Lady Cust with her niece Caroline, Benjamin West, c.1770. Jocosa was the sister-in-law of Mary Anne Drury who married the 2nd Earl in 1761; Caroline was his second daughter and the future Lady Suffield (d.1850). There is a smaller but identical picture at Belton. The Maratta frame is contemporary.
An Unknown Girl, English, 17th century.
George III and Queen Charlotte, studio of Allan Ramsay, 1763. State portraits painted as part of Lord Buckinghamshire's panoply for his St Petersburg Embassy, in good contemporary frames.

FURNITURE

Around the walls is a set of eight chairs and two sofas, c.1780. The silk is a 1984 reweaving of Lord Lothian's damask, itself a revival of a 19th-century French pattern.
Two mahogany side-tables, Chippendale, c.1740.
Louis XV-style writing-table with gilt mounts, 19th century.
Louis XV kingwood commode, of *bombé* form with gilt mounts, early 18th century.
Two lacquered cabinets on stands, oriental, late 18th century. In the centre of the room, a duet stool covered with a piece of Beauvais tapestry which was part of some early 19th-century curtains.
Low table with X-framed legs. The laquered top may have formed part of a late 17th-century cabinet.
Oak gateleg table, early 18th century.

CLOCK

Eight-day mantel regulation in a sycamore case by Weeks of London, c.1815.

CERAMICS

Three large Japanese Imari jars, 18th century.

TEXTILES

Curtains of cream rayon brocatelle lined with taffeta of shot peach and green with inner curtains of shot taffeta, 1930s.
The large sofas are covered in satin striped rayon.
Indian carpet, 19th century. Made at the prison in Agra where the absence of the profit motive and rigorous inspection ensured very high standards.

THE UPPER ANTE ROOM

Originally the upper part of the Jacobean staircase, this space became an ante room hung with tapestries in 1767. In the 19th century it was used as a billiard room. The bookcases were installed in the 1930s when the books were moved up from the Lower Ante Room.

CEILING

A fine early 17th-century design of straps radiating from a central carved wooden boss which was executed by Robert Lyminge himself and originally hung over the stairwell.

DOORS AND DADOS

These were installed in 1767. Above cartouches with the Hobart bull is a panel of heavy geometrical ornaments simulating Jacobean work.

TAPESTRIES

The set was made at the Mortlake factory started by Francis Crane in 1619 under the patronage of James I. This series was woven after 1657 when Philip Hollieburie petitioned the Commonwealth Council for permission to weave 'The History of Abraham'. They are based on a similar set woven at Brussels between 1530 and 1540 by Bernaert van Orley and now at Hampton Court. The borders were probably designed by Francis Cleyn. The subjects are:

The parting of Abraham from Lot at Bethel; Sarah sending her Egyptian maidservant Hagar away with the infant Ishmael; Melchisadek offering bread and wine to Abraham after the slaughter of Chedorlaomer and the kings that were with him; a soldier with a lance; King Abimelech; Sarah; King Abimelech taking Sarah from Abraham.

The three single figures are additions by the Mortlake factory but the other scenes are drawn from the ten large tapestries in the Brussels set. The tapestries are the subject of a 12-year conservation programme by the Blickling textile workroom.

CARPET

An important Axminster carpet of the late 18th century with Palladian guilloche border and a floral centrepiece.

FURNITURE

Lacquered chest on stand, oriental, 18th century.
Four high-back chairs, mid 17th century, with 'Norwich Red' moreen cushions, c.1800.
Two Chinese Chippendale silver tables with fret galleries.
Desk, early 19th century.

CERAMICS

Garniture de Cheminée, decorated with views, Barr, Flight and Barr, Worcester, c.1814.
Two fine *famille verte* Kangxi dishes, one of which came with the house; the other was given in 1974.
Nodding mandarin, oriental, late 19th century.

BRONZES

Silenus holding the Infant Bacchus and *Venus and Cupid*, ? French c.1700.

CLOCK

Eight-day English skeleton clock, c.1860.

STAIRCASE GALLERY

Formed in 1767 when the front wall of the Great Hall was moved outwards into the courtyard. At the same time the two richly carved Jacobean doorcases were moved here from positions on the old staircase.

PICTURES

? *Sir Thomas Sebright, 4th Baronet* (1692–1736) or *Mr Crawley*, William Aikman (page 78).
Henry Kelsall (1692–1762) of Colkirk, Norfolk, William Aikman, 1729. Senior Clerk at the Treasury, he is identified by a letter in his right hand.

Drawing for the remodelling of the Great Hall, William Ivory, 1765.

FURNITURE

Cassone, 19th century, incorporating three mid 15th-century Florentine panel paintings. LEFT-HAND PANEL: The rape of Dejanira, with Hercules drawing his bow at Nessus; RIGHT-HAND PANEL: Hercules slaying the Nemean Lion; CENTRAL PANEL: Three unidentified kings drawn in chariots in a triumphal procession.
Two high-back chairs with cushions of 'Norwich Red' moreen, English, 17th century.
Two oak hall chairs with cabriole legs, Victorian.

CERAMIC

A vase by the Martin Brothers, late 19th century.

THE LONG GALLERY

The Jacobean Long Gallery, 123 feet in length, was used by the 1st Earl for the display of his series of full-length portraits (page 29). The equestrian portrait of George II (now in the Peter the Great Room) may have hung on the end wall. The room became a library c.1745 with the inheritance of the Ellys books (page 30), and the Haymans (page 82) were painted as overdoors for it. Between 1858 and 1863 its decoration was transformed once more by the 8th Marquis of Lothian.

PLASTERWORK

Edward Stanyon carried out the intricate pattern of embossed ribs, studded with pendants delineating 31 major panels. The 11 central panels contain five heraldic achievements and symbols of the Five Senses and of Learning ('Doctrina'). The latter image and the series of 20 emblems which run down either side of the ceiling were chosen from Henry Peacham's *Minerva Britanna* of 1612 (page 22). Copies of the relevant plates and the accompanying texts may be examined by visitors. In certain parts of the frieze (especially over the fireplace) it is possible to detect sections of 18th-century plasterwork carefully arranged to match the old work. This was probably the work of 'Newman Plaisterer' to whom the 1st Earl paid £44 9s 3d for work in the Long Gallery shortly after 1745.

THE FIREPLACE

The Siena marble fireplace for which Joseph Pickford was paid no less than £192 13s 5d in the mid 1740s (page 30) was replaced in 1858–63 by a huge hooded stone chimney-piece (page 44) which was, in turn, removed by the 11th Marquis in the 1930s. The spectacular iron firedogs were made by Joshua Hart and Sons to the specification of Pollen, who may also have designed the cast iron fireback. The fire-irons and the twisted bar were the work of the estate blacksmith John Salmon (page 63). The wooden bolection surround was installed in 1972.

THE PAINTED FRIEZE

This is entirely the work of J. H. Pollen (page 44) though the boards on which it is painted are possibly part of the room's mid 18th-century fittings. The panel over the book cupboard door was painted by Anna Wellbourne in 1975–76, when the frieze, which had faded badly, was restored and retouched. The 11th Marquis obscured Pollen's painted decoration on the window recesses.

STAINED GLASS

The upper lights of the north window contain heraldic panels executed in 1861 by Powells of Whitefriars to designs by J. H. Pollen. From left to right the arms are Jedburgh, Ancram, Lothian, Hobart and Britiffe. The glass is surprisingly broadly handled for its date; in this, and in its deliberate use of unevenly coloured pieces, it anticipates Arts and Crafts stained glass.

BOOKCASES

Designed by Benjamin Woodward and carved by John O'Shea with naturalistic foliage, they incorporate the carcasses of the 1st Earl's bookcases. The carving is unfinished (page 45) and preliminary cutting out on the side of one press near the south end shows how much more was proposed.

THE BOOKS

(*See Chapter 5*)

THE FLOOR

The patterned border, now much worn, is by Pollen.

TAPESTRY

Jacob and Esau, Brussels, mid 17th century.

PICTURES

AROUND THE FIREPLACE
Four portraits on copper of *Edward VI*, *Mary I*, *Richard III* and *Elizabeth I*, late 18th century.

FURNITURE

At the south end is a chair of state recorded in the 1793 inventory for the South Drawing Room as 'The Chair of State in which King James II sat when in Ireland – given to Lord Buckinghamshire by the Earl of Clanbrassil'. At some stage it has been deprived of its tasselled cushions, shorn of its fringes and re-covered.

Two large chests, one 17th century and decorated with pokerwork, the other an oriental lacquered chest of the early 18th century.

IN THE WINDOW BAYS
Two mahogany library tables with Chinese Chippendale brackets, probably part of the 1st Earl's library furnishings.
Oval gateleg tables, early 18th century.
Low-backed Windsor chairs with cabriole legs, late 18th century.
Mahogany benches with multiple legs and contemporary 'Norwich Red' moreen tops, early 19th century. They become library steps when set on end.
Armchair with swept legs and cane seat, also converts into library steps, early 19th century.

IN FRONT OF THE PRESSES
Low spindle-backed chairs also upholstered in 'Norwich Red', late 18th century.

NEAR THE FIREPLACE
Four stick-backed Windsor chairs; sophisticated late 18th-century mahogany versions of their rustic prototypes. They could be some of the '6 wood bottomed chairs' that furnished Lady's Cottage (page 68).
Two low ebony stools, early 19th century; recovered in 1977 with an exact copy of the original covers.
Rosewood folio stand designed to hold drawings, engravings and maps, early 19th century.

PIANO

Forte-piano by Joseph Kirkman in rosewood case, 1829.

THE TURRET STAIRCASE

The upper part was a closet to the Long Gallery and has a fine Jacobean ceiling with the Hobart bull in the centre. The panelling is *c*.1730, and the staircase was inserted in 1773 to communicate between the Library and Lord Buckinghamshire's Study beneath.

THE PETER THE GREAT ROOM

Work on the fitting out of the Peter the Great Room took place 1778–82.

CEILING

William Wilkins of Norwich, grandfather of the architect, executed the plasterwork to William Ivory's drawings. The design derives from the illusionistic ceilings discovered in Pompeii and Herculaneum in the mid 18th century, some of which had octagonal centres and rising tabernacles occupying the corners. The latter are represented in flattened and simplified form in the irregular pentagonal corner compartments. The Hobart bulls are displayed in medallions at either end with Lord Buckinghamshire's arms in the centre. The masks of the frieze imitate Jacobean ornaments.

THE FIREPLACE

In 1778 John Ivory was paid 100 guineas for the 'statuary sienna chimneypiece'. The grate, surround, fender and fire-irons are contemporary.

DECORATION

This room was redecorated in 1987. The ceiling is recorded in 1806 as 'having the four corner compartments with that in the middle . . . stained a delicate pink' and this, together with the colour of the wall hanging, has formed the basis of the present scheme. The new silk and worsted 'half damask' has been copied from surviving fragments of the 18th-century silk and woven to the original 21-inch width on the handlooms at De Vere Mills, Castle Hedingham, Essex. The unusual pattern, a vertical stripe composed of continuous floral garlands and sprigs of lily of the valley, is more commonly found on dress fabrics of the 1760s. Dress, being more ephemeral than wall hangings, was the main vehicle for change in textile patterns at this period.

The curtains were described in the 1793 inventory as '3 Festoon Window curtains like the Hanging of the Room'.

FURNITURE

The furnishing of the room corresponds almost exactly to the 1793 inventory: '2 cabriole sophas; 4 Pillows; 4 Elbow Chairs; 10 small Do cover'd the same as the Room with strip'd Manchester Cases; 4 Needlework Stools and Cases as above', and is laid out formally as it would have been in the 2nd Earl's time.

The seat furniture is typical of the designs which Hepplewhite was to publish in his *Cabinet-maker and Upholsterer's Guide* of 1788, although surprisingly for a room of such grandeur they are executed in plain mahogany.

The three large pier-glasses with their gilt Maratta frames and heraldic crestings, the frames of the Gainsboroughs and the even larger frame of the tapestry were all supplied by Solomon Hudson of Great Titchfield Street, London, who was paid the huge sum of £406 6s 6d in 1782 for these and two more in the State Bedroom.

Only the marble of the two pier-tables described in 1793 survives. The frames were renewed by William Freeman and Company of Norwich in the early 19th century.

TAPESTRY

The tapestry of *Peter the Great triumphing over the defeated Swedish army at Poltawa in 1709* was given to the 2nd Earl by Catherine the Great at the end of his Embassy in 1765. Woven at St Petersburg in 1764, it relates to a tapestry of 1722, now in the Hermitage, Leningrad, which is based on a design by the Russian court painter Louis Caravaque. The Blickling tapestry has a more detailed background and a border of coats of arms lacking in the 1722 version. Much of the detail is fine but there are also coarse passages; the St Petersburg factory, set up by Peter the Great and revived by Catherine, was staffed jointly by Parisian weavers from the Gobelins factory and less experienced Russian apprentices.

CARPET

The Axminster, which can only have been made for this room, is a mixture of old-fashioned and up-to-date motifs. The red guilloche border resembles a Palladian ceiling of the mid 18th century while the centrepiece, the garlands, bouquets and large rosettes are more reminiscent of the 1770s.

PICTURES

ON THE EAST WALL

King George II on horseback, John Wootton and Charles Jervas. Painted shortly before 1732 when it was described by George Vertue:

'The Queen attended with Several Noblemen came . . . to Mr Wottons in Cavendish Square to see . . . a great picture of his Majesty painted on horseback a grey horse for Lord Hubbard the face of the King by Mr Jarvis & all other parts by Mr Wooton – the Horse &c. was much approv'd off, but the Kings not thought to be like, was much spoke against from thence.'

ON EITHER SIDE OF THE FIREPLACE

John Hobart, 2nd Earl of Buckinghamshire in his robes of the Lord Lieutenant of Ireland, and *Caroline Conolly* (his second wife), Thomas Gainsborough, 1784.

CHANDELIER

Sixteen-light Waterford crystal chandelier introduced between 1793 and 1806.

ON THE MANTELPIECE

Two Waterford crystal lustres, late 18th century.

CLOCK

Eight-day French striking mantel clock, *c*.1820, in an ormolu and red marble case. The movement is stamped 'Hemon, a Paris'.

THE STATE BEDROOM

William Ivory submitted drawings for the frieze and cornice of the 'State Dressing room' in April 1779 but it seems unlikely that these plans were acceptable to Lord Buckinghamshire and Samuel Wyatt may have been asked to design this room in about 1780 (page 40). The placing of the state bed behind the pillars of an alcove is a deliberately archaic arrangement appropriate to a room intended as an inner sanctum, reflecting not only the prestige of the then owner but also the fact that Blickling was founded by James I's Lord Chief Justice whose portrait was the only picture here in 1793. The carved wooden frieze of swags and ox masks refers to the Jacobean decoration of the entrance front and the Hobart crest.

FIREPLACE

The marble surround is different in character from John Ivory's fireplaces in other rooms both in its ornament and the balance of its colours – pure white marble with Siena plaques. The burnished steel register stove, fender and fire-irons are contemporary.

DECORATION

The present hangings, which are close to the colour of original fragments, date from 1981. The crimson braid is a feature of the original decoration.

PICTURE

Sir Henry Hobart, 1st Baronet, Daniel Mytens. Sir Henry's account book records a part payment on 22 December 1624 of £5 10s 0d to 'Mr Daniell Mittens the picture drawer . . . for ye drawing of yr Lor[dshi]ps picture'. Although the pose is conventional the portrait is painted with great sensitivity and is among Mytens' finest works.

FURNITURE

The white and gilt polescreen and octagonal table are part of the original furnishings. The latter has an interesting top: a design on paper under glass, similar to a late Roman ceiling. The suite of white and gilt chairs and stools is described in the 1793 inventory and is similar in design to the contemporary but less ornate mahogany suite in the Peter the Great Room.

The fine serpentine commode of *bombé* form with ormolu mounts to the left of the fireplace and the similar dressing-table on the opposite side of the room are probably by John Cobb who was paid £86 in 1762 by Lord Buckinghamshire for unspecified items.

The tester and headboard of the bed are made up of a canopy of state issued to Lord Buckinghamshire in 1763 for his embassy to St Petersburg and made by William Vile and John Cobb. The arms of George II appear on the headboard but those on the counterpane are Queen Anne's. Two different damasks are used.

The two commodes on either side of the bed are also likely to be Cobb's work.

The looking-glasses above them have rich rococo frames, 1760s.

The pier-table is listed in the 1793 inventory. The glass above it was made, together with the frame for Sir Henry Hobart's portrait, by Solomon Hudson in 1782 (page 89).

CARPET

Axminster, made for this room and one of the superlative examples of its period. Its design partly reflects the garlanded foliage of the ceiling but the strong black border with its swags of flowers and crimson lines is related to Roman mural decoration.

The contemporary bed carpet, of three strips sewn together, is a rare survival. The only other one is at Osterley Park.

CERAMICS

ON THE DRESSING-TABLE
Two enamel candlesticks, Bilston c.1760.
Pair of bowls with covers, Rockingham, 18th century.

ON THE COMMODES TO EITHER SIDE OF THE BED
Two elaborate vases garlanded with flowers, Meissen, 19th century.

METALWORK

Two gilt and bronze candelabra in the form of putti, early 19th century.

STAIRCASE

The staircase was built in 1967. The plaster ceiling and dado panelling of the former State Bedroom closet remain in the upper part.

DOCUMENT ROOM

This was the bedroom of the 11th Marquis in the 1930s and is now used for the display of documents, books, drawings and other memorabilia relating to him and to Blickling.

FAMILY TREE

Owners of Blickling appear in CAPITALS

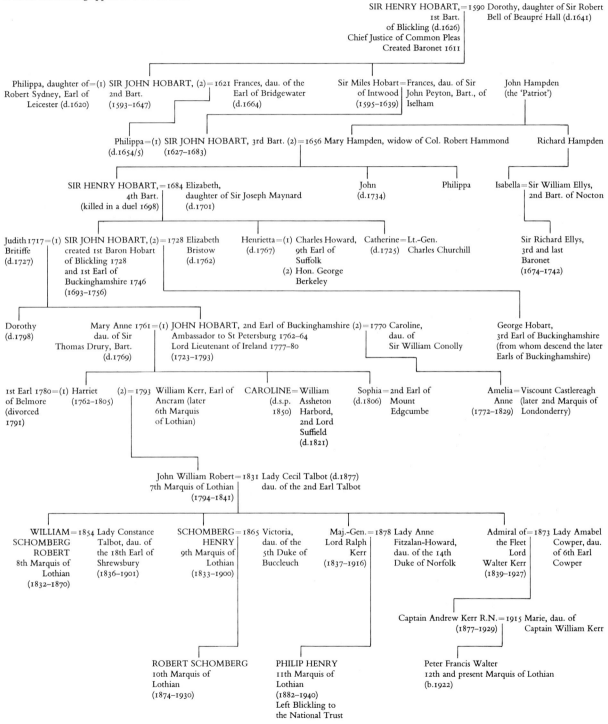

SIR HENRY HOBART, =1590 Dorothy, daughter of Sir Robert
1st Bart. Bell of Beaupré Hall (d.1641)
of Blickling (d.1626)
Chief Justice of Common Pleas
Created Baronet 1611

Philippa, daughter of=(1) SIR JOHN HOBART, (2)=1621 Frances, dau. of the Sir Miles Hobart=Frances, dau. of Sir John Hampden
Robert Sydney, Earl of 2nd Bart. Earl of Bridgewater of Intwood | John Peyton, Bart., of (the 'Patriot')
Leicester (d.1620) (1593–1647) (d.1664) (1595–1639) | Iselham

Philippa=(1) SIR JOHN HOBART, 3rd Bart. (2)=1656 Mary Hampden, widow of Col. Robert Hammond Richard Hampden
(d.1654/5) (1627–1683)

SIR HENRY HOBART,=1684 Elizabeth, John Philippa Isabella=Sir William Ellys,
4th Bart. daughter of Sir Joseph Maynard (d.1734) 2nd Bart. of Nocton
(killed in a duel 1698) (d.1701)

Judith 1717=(1) SIR JOHN HOBART, (2)=1728 Elizabeth Henrietta=(1) Charles Howard, Catherine=Lt.-Gen. Sir Richard Ellys,
Britiffe created 1st Baron Hobart Bristow (d.1767) 9th Earl of (d.1725) Charles Churchill 3rd and last
(d.1727) of Blickling 1728 (d.1762) Suffolk Baronet
and 1st Earl of (2) Hon. George (1674–1742)
Buckinghamshire 1746 Berkeley
(1693–1756)

Dorothy Mary Anne 1761=(1) JOHN HOBART, 2nd Earl of Buckinghamshire (2)=1770 Caroline, George Hobart,
(d.1798) dau. of Sir Ambassador to St Petersburg 1762–64 dau. of 3rd Earl of Buckinghamshire
Thomas Drury, Bart. Lord Lieutenant of Ireland 1777–80 Sir William Conolly (from whom descend the later
(d.1769) (1723–1793) Earls of Buckinghamshire)

1st Earl 1780=(1) Harriet (2)=1793 William Kerr, Earl of CAROLINE=William Sophia=2nd Earl of Amelia=Viscount Castlereagh
of Belmore (1762–1805) Ancram (later (d.s.p. Assheton (d.1806) Mount Anne (later 2nd Marquis of
(divorced 6th Marquis 1850) Harbord, Edgcumbe (1772–1829) Londonderry)
1791) of Lothian) 2nd Lord
Suffield
(d.1821)

John William Robert=1831 Lady Cecil Talbot (d.1877)
7th Marquis of Lothian dau. of the 2nd Earl Talbot
(1794–1841)

WILLIAM=1854 Lady Constance SCHOMBERG=1865 Victoria, Maj.-Gen.=1878 Lady Anne Admiral of=1873 Lady Amabel
SCHOMBERG Talbot, dau. of HENRY dau. of the Lord Ralph Fitzalan-Howard, the Fleet | Cowper, dau.
ROBERT the 18th Earl of 9th Marquis of 5th Duke of Kerr dau. of the 14th Lord | of 6th Earl
8th Marquis of Shrewsbury Lothian Buccleuch (1837–1916) Duke of Norfolk Walter Kerr | Cowper
Lothian (1836–1901) (1833–1900) (1839–1927)
(1832–1870)

Captain Andrew Kerr R.N.=1915 Marie, dau. of
(1877–1929) Captain William Kerr

ROBERT SCHOMBERG PHILIP HENRY Peter Francis Walter
10th Marquis of 11th Marquis of 12th and present Marquis of Lothian
Lothian Lothian (b.1922)
(1874–1930) (1882–1940)
Left Blickling to
the National Trust

PLANS OF THE HOUSE

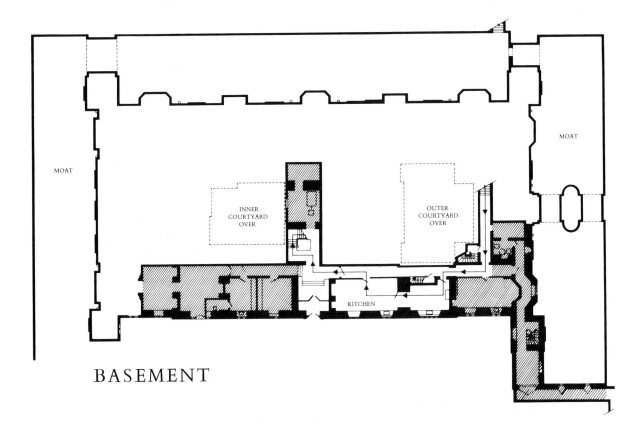

MOAT

MOAT

INNER
COURTYARD
OVER

OUTER
COURTYARD
OVER

KITCHEN

BASEMENT

N

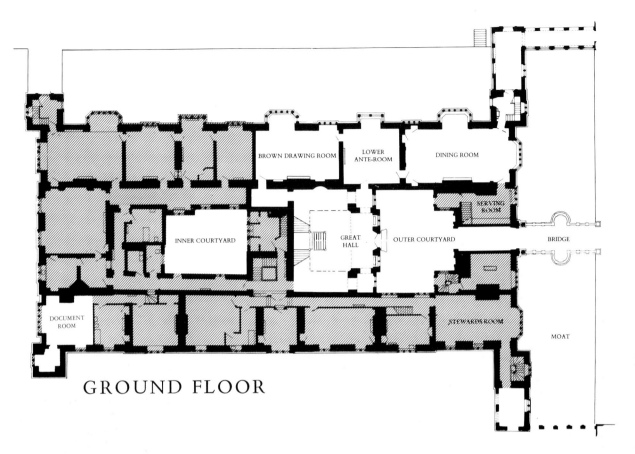

GROUND FLOOR

BROWN DRAWING ROOM

LOWER ANTE-ROOM

DINING ROOM

SERVING ROOM

INNER COURTYARD

GREAT HALL

OUTER COURTYARD

BRIDGE

DOCUMENT ROOM

STEWARDS ROOM

MOAT

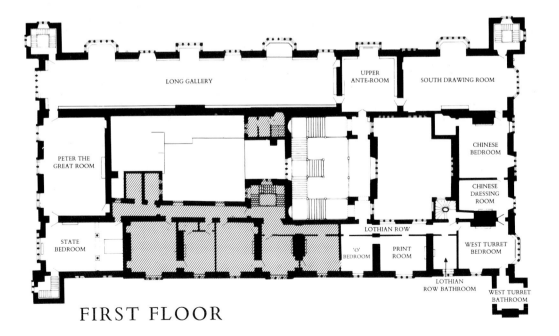

FIRST FLOOR

LONG GALLERY

UPPER ANTE-ROOM

SOUTH DRAWING ROOM

CHINESE BEDROOM

PETER THE GREAT ROOM

CHINESE DRESSING ROOM

LOTHIAN ROW

STATE BEDROOM

'O' BEDROOM

PRINT ROOM

WEST TURRET BEDROOM

LOTHIAN ROW BATHROOM

WEST TURRET BATHROOM

BIBLIOGRAPHY

The Hobart and Lothian family papers are deposited in the Norfolk and Norwich Record Office.

BARTELL, E., *Cromer Considered as a Watering Place*, 2nd edition, 1806.

BEATNIFFE, R., *The Norfolk Tour or Traveller's Pocket Companion*, 1795.

BLOMEFIELD, F., *Essay towards a Topographical History of Norfolk*, Vol. III, 1769.

BUTLER, J. R. M., *Lord Lothian, 1882–1940*, 1960.

COLLYER, A. D'Arcy, *The Despatches and Correspondence of John, second Earl of Buckinghamshire, Ambassador to the Court of Catherine II of Russia*, 2 vols, 1900.

DRAPER, M. P. G., *Marble Hill House and its owners*, 1970.

CROKER, J. W., *Lady Suffolk's Letters*, 1824.

EVANS, M. C., 'The Descendents of Thomas Ivory', *Norfolk Archaeology*, Vol. XXIX, part II, 1985, pp. 206–213.

FISHER, G. and SMITH, H., 'John Hungerford Pollen and his decorative work at Blickling Hall' in *The National Trust Year Book*, 1975–76.

GRIGG, Sir E., 'Philip Kerr Marquis of Lothian', a memoir in *The American Speeches of Lord Lothian*, 1941.

HARRIS, J., 'The Prideaux Collection of Topographical Drawings', *Architectural History*, Vol. VII, 1963.

Historical Manuscripts Commission, *Report on the manuscripts of the Marquis of Lothian preserved at Blickling Hall, Norfolk*, 1905.

HUSSEY, C., 'Blickling Hall' in *Country Life*, 7, 21 and 28 June, 1930.

KETTON-CREMER, R. W., *Norfolk Portraits*, 1944, and *Norfolk Assembly*, 1957.

LEES-MILNE, J., *Ancestral Voices*, 1975; *Prophesying Peace*, 1977.

MEYRICK, M. H., *Historical Notes and Guide to Blickling Hall and Blickling Church*, 1924.

PHIBBS, J. L., *Blickling Park Survey*, 1981; an unpublished study held at Blickling.

POLLEN, A., *John Hungerford Pollen 1820–1902*, 1912.

REYNOLDS, D., 'Lord Lothian and Anglo-American Relations 1939–1940', *Transactions of the American Philosophical Society*, Vol. 73, part 2, 1983.

SAPWELL, J., *A History of Aylsham*, 1960.

STANLEY-MILLSON, C. and NEWMAN, J., 'Blickling Hall: the Building of a Jacobean Mansion', *Architectural History*, Vol. 29, 1986, pp. 1–43.

SUTCLIFFE, J. H. F. H., 'A Statue of Diana at Blickling', *Norfolk Archaeology*, Vol. XXXV, 1970, p. 144.

Blickling Hall, lately injured by fire, from *The Illustrated London News*, 31 October 1874

INDEX